The Portable Postmodernist

Arthur Asa Berger

ALTAMIRA
PRESS

A Division of
ROWMAN & LITTLEFIELD PUBLISHERS, INC.
Walnut Creek • Lanham • New York • Oxford

AltaMira Press
A Division of Rowman & Littlefield Publishers, Inc.
1630 North Main Street, #367
Walnut Creek, CA 94596
www.altamirapress.com

Rowman & Littlefield Publishers, Inc.
A Member of the Rowman & Littlefield Publishing Group
4501 Forbes Boulevard, Suite 200
Lanham, MD 20706

PO Box 317
Oxford
OX2 9RU, UK

British Library Cataloguing in Publication Information Available

Library of Congress Cataloging-in-Publication Data

Berger, Arthur Asa, 1933–
    The portable postmodernist / Arthur Asa Berger.
        p. cm.
    Includes bibliographical references and index.
    ISBN 0-7591-0313-5 (alk. paper) — ISBN 0-7591-0314-3 (pbk. : alk. paper)
    1. Postmodernism. I. Title.
    B831.2 .B465 2003
    149'.97—dc21   2002014297

Printed in the United States of America

♾™ The paper used in this publication meets the minimum requirements of American National Standard for Information Sciences—Permanence of Paper for Printed Library Materials, ANSI/NISO Z39.48–1992.

Contents

Introduction

There are countless books by postmodernists (and those who attack postmodernism as nonsense) on its impact on our buildings, novels, paintings, films, fashion, and so on. If you go to a search engine such as Google and type in "postmodernism," you will find approximately 145,000 web pages where various aspects of postmodernism are dealt with. We see the term mentioned in newspapers and newsmagazines all the time now, and it is likely that many people now have a vague idea of what postmodernism (also known as "pomo" or "po-mo") is. But it is a difficult term to pin down.

Postmodernism is like a piece of wet soap that keeps slipping out of your hands; you think you have it and then it slides away from you. In an effort to give you a better idea of what postmodernism is and what its impact has been on our culture (and other cultures as well), I have created a postmodern book—or in the jargon of literary theorists, "text." This book is a pastiche, an assemblage, a collection of fragments, the literary equivalent of a form of art known as a collage, in which you will find quotations from postmodernists and scholars of postmodernism to give you a better idea of what postmodernism is. And isn't. You may even think of this book as a kind of literary installation, in which you can wander through an area and make some interesting discoveries. I have also written commentaries that go with each selection to help you understand the significance of each selection and, in some cases, the implications of the ideas in the selection.

What This Book Deals With

In this book I will deal such topics as:

1. What is postmodernism? (which means literally the period coming *after* modernism)
2. What is modernism? (the period coming *before* postmodernism)
3. What impact has postmodernism had on our lives and beliefs and our societies?
4. What are some of the most interesting ideas of postmodernist thinkers?
5. What issues does postmodernism raise?

In this introduction, I will consider each of these subjects briefly, as a means of providing a map to what we might describe as the postmodern territory—which, you will see, is enormous and without very highly defined boundaries.

1. What Is *Postmodernism?*

I start with the notion that people who grow up in postmodern societies are, somehow, different from those who grow up in modernist societies or in earlier traditional, premodern societies. To understand why, we have to understand something about postmodernism. Literally speaking, the term means "coming after" modernism. So postmodernism is defined in terms of time periods. "Post" means "after," but it can also suggest "moving beyond," "different from," or "the opposite of."

Generally speaking, the modernist period is held to have occurred between approximately 1900 and 1960. The postmodernist period, then, involves the years between 1960 and the present, roughly speaking—though there are some scholars and theorists who would suggest we are now, and have been for a number of years, in a *post*-postmodernist period. Other scholars argue that what we call postmodernism is actually a kind of modernism.

There is a great debate on postmodernism that permeates our universities and culture, in general. This book can be seen as a postmodern (in form) contribution to this debate. Critics of postmodernism claim it is one more passing fad (or one more fad that has already passed) popularized by French and other intellectuals, while defenders of postmodernism argue that we are now in a different world, a postmodern world, and that postmodernism and postmodernist theory are necessary to explain that world. That is, postmodernist thinkers argue that there has been a sudden "cultural mutation," and this mutation, this remarkable change in beliefs, attitudes, philosophies, and aesthetic sensibilities, is what is explained by postmodernism.

One of the first modern scholars to use the term was the famous British historian Arnold Toynbee. We find the term mentioned in a one-volume condensation, by D. C. Somervell, of the first six volumes of Toynbee's epic work, *A Study of History.*

Around 1960, scholars started using the term "postmodernism" more and more. Thus, we find Bernard Rosenberg, a sociologist, mentioning the term in an introduction he wrote to *Mass Culture*: "First besieged with commodities, postmodern man himself becomes an interchangeable part in the whole cultural process." (1957: 4). Rosenberg ties postmodernism to the mass media and the rise of consumer culture, a relationship that other postmodernist theorists have also dealt with and expanded upon. He sees the media and postmodernism as leading to a kind of worldwide cultural homogenization, which is at odds with the contemporary view that postmodernism involves a kind hyperdifferentiation in people—with everyone doing his or her "own thing," to use a phrase once popular but now seldom heard.

One of the best short descriptions of postmodernism appears in Ellis Cashmore and Chris Rojek's anthology, *Dictionary of Cultural Theorists*. In the editors' introduction to the book, they explain that in postmodernity, what seemed to be fixed and universal categories and certainty are replaced by a focus on difference, that there no longer are any agreed-upon cultural boundaries or certainties, and that we have abandoned a belief in scientific rationality and all-embracing theories of truth and of progress (1999: 6).

We find this notion explicated in the first selection in this book, in which Jean-François Lyotard explains that people in postmodern societies no longer have faith in what he calls "metanarratives," the overarching philosophical beliefs that used to give people notions of what is important and how to live.

Cashmore and Rojek discuss another important aspect of postmodernist thought—its sense that concepts take their meaning from the relations in which they are embedded. They point out that it is the relations that exist among things (and, we can add, among people) that are crucial, that generate meaning. This last notion, that nothing has meaning in itself and that meaning stems from relationships, was elaborated in 1915 in Ferdinand de Saussure's posthumously published book, *Course in General Linguistics*. In chapter 16, I quote an important passage in this book where Saussure explains how language shapes the way we think about concepts.

Cashmore and Rojek also offer a discussion of some of the implications of postmodernism for our attitudes toward elite and popular culture and the importance of intertextuality, among other things. The modernist beliefs in hierarchy and the difference between high culture and low or popular culture are no longer accepted, and human relations are seen as fragmentary and changeable. We live in a world in which simulation is all-important—in which real objects are replaced by their copies and in which culture has to be seen as an assemblage of texts, all of which are intertextually related to one another and gain their meaning from their connection to other texts that preceded them (1999: 6–7).

Let me add an important point here. From the postmodernist perspective, everything is a "text" to be read and analyzed, and everything gains its meaning from its relation to other texts. The term "intertextuality" refers to the idea that texts are all shaped, to various degrees, by other texts that preceded them. Sometimes the borrowing is unconscious and sometimes it is consciously done, as in parodies, in which we ridicule a well-known text, a popular genre, or a distinctive style of writing.

The impact of intertextuality, Cashmore and Rojek suggest, is to weaken our belief in the importance of originality and to emphasize the degree to which we must read people, events, and objects by seeing their relationships with other people, events, and objects. And that is because all meaning comes from seeing relationships, from recognizing that nothing has meaning in itself and that we find meaning by relating our experiences to texts, in all media, with which we are familiar (1999: 6-7).

2. What Is Modernism?

The term "modern" comes from the fifth-century Latin word *modernus*, which was used to differentiate the pagan era from the Christian era. As Bryan S. Turner explains in his book *Theories of Modernity and Postmodernity,* we can equate modernism with a rejection of history and with the notion of differentiation, which means, then, that postmodernism involves a kind of cultural dedifferentiation. Postmodernism develops at the same time that consumer capitalism becomes dominant, and thus postmodernism is associated with a world in which consumer culture and mass consumption dominate fashion and shape people's lifestyles. We live now in a world dominated by media and images and simulations of reality; this world of signs has undermined our sense of reality and dissolved our sense that there are fixed structures and stable boundaries, that anything has meaning (1991: 3–4). Like so many belief systems, postmodernism is intimately connected to the system it rejected and replaced—modernism.

Let me summarize now some of the differences between postmodernism and modernism, which have been mentioned or implied in the discussion above. First, if modernism involves differentiation (between the elite arts and popular culture), postmodernism involves what can be described as dedifferentiation, breaking down the barriers between the elite arts and popular culture and reveling joyfully in mass culture. If modernism involves a "high seriousness" toward life, postmodernism involves an element of game playing and an ironic stance as well as a kind of playfulness. In postmodernist societies, people "play" with their identities, changing them when they feel bored with their old ones.

If modernism involves stylistic purity, as reflected visually in modernist architecture, postmodernism involves stylistic eclecticism and variety, with the pastiche as the governing metaphor. If modernism believes we can know reality, postmodernism argues that we are all confounded by illusions and hyperreality. Postmodernism is the realm of consumer culture, in contrast to what we might call the production culture of modernism. The heroes of modernism are the great businessmen and statesmen, while the heroes of postmodernism tend to be celebrities and entertainment figures, whose tastes and consumption habits are held up as models to us all. At the end of this book you will find several highly elaborated charts that deal with the differences between modernism and postmodernism in considerable detail.

3. What Impact Has Postmodernism Had on Our Lives and Beliefs and Our Societies?

If postmodern theory were some interesting notion that philosophers debated about but which had little or no impact on our everyday lives, it probably wouldn't have achieved the notoriety is has. The argument of postmodernist theorists is that postmodernism represents a cultural "mutation," and this mutation has affected many aspects of our societies and our lives, whether or not we are aware of this being the case.

Take, for example, the matter of architecture. In his book *After the Great Divide: Modernism, Mass Culture, Postmodernism*, Andreas Huyssen writes that it is in architecture that we see most clearly how postmodernism has broken away from modernism. He offers the example of the great Dutch architect Ludwig Mies van der Rohe, whose "glass curtain walls" differ profoundly from the work of postmodern architects, with their use of mixed styles. He cites as a typical postmodern building Philip Johnson's famous AT&T skyscraper, which has a Roman colonnade at its street level, a neoclassical midsection, and a Chippendale pediment at its top. This postmodern eclecticism is also found in literature, the arts, film, and mass culture in recent years (1986: 184–85).

Architecture, like all the arts, feeds on certain sensibilities that are found in a given time period. In this case, the Johnson building is a repudiation of modernist architecture, with its monotonous slabs of windows and an extreme simplification of style. Las Vegas, so the critics tell us, is a city where the eclecticism shown in the Johnson building is found permeating the whole Strip. And postmodernist architects tell us that we can learn a great deal from Las Vegas. The same sensibility found in the Johnson building, the same desire for newness and eclecticism, affects music, painting, drama, film, many other arts, and the way we live our lives, as well. And that is because these arts, I would suggest, have an impact on our individual psyches and affect the way we think about things and lead our lives.

We must always remember that, as the great French sociologist Émile Durkheim pointed out, we all have a dual relationship with society: *we are in society* (as individuals, leading our own lives) and *society is in us* (which explains where we get ideas about everything from what kind of clothes to wear to whether or not we should get an education, what our occupation should be, and so on, ad infinitum).

Where we are born has important implications for our attitudes, our food preferences, and many other things. The American notion of the self-made man and self-made woman is, we must remember, not something we are born with. We get this notion from growing up in America, where many of the novels we read and other stories we are exposed to affirm this notion. If you were to take a baby born in the United States and bring it to Vietnam for its first twenty years, the person you get would be considerably different than if you were to take a baby born in Vietnam and bring it to the United States for its first twenty years. In short, human beings are social animals and are profoundly affected by the societies in which they grow up and live. It is only natural, then, that a person born in the United States after 1960 would have a considerably different sensibility than a person born in 1920 or 1930. I'm not talking about generational differences here, but something deeper—a different mind-set and a different (that is, a postmodern) notion of how to live.

That explains why in this book you will find selections dealing with romantic love in postmodern societies, advertising and postmodernism, therapy and postmodernism, Disney and postmodernism, punk and postmodernism, African Americans and postmodernism, and a number of other analyses, all of which suggest that life in postmodern societies is radically different than it was before 1960, which we are taking as a cutoff point between modernist and postmodernist societies.

4. The Ideas of Selected Postmodernist Thinkers

This could easily be a book-length discussion. When you mention the word "postmodernism" and ask what it means, you are asking for a very long and complicated story. This book, actually, is on that subject—as postmodernism (and modernism) relate to a number of different aspects of life in the United States and other postmodern countries. What I will offer in this introduction is a sampling of some of the thinkers represented in the book and some of the concepts they deal with that are generally associated with postmodernism and modernism. I let the authors I have selected flesh out the discussion of each topic in considerably more detail in the book. I will deal primarily here with the first ten selections in the book.

I start the book with one of the seminal statements of postmodernism, by Jean-François Lyotard. He discusses a core notion of postmodernism—a disbelief in the validity of the old narratives and the moral absolutes that stemmed from them that used to govern our thinking in modernist and premodernist periods. I quote him later on his analysis of postmodernism's fascination with the eclectic— the desire postmodernists have to mix various styles in fashion, food, architecture, literature, and lifestyle in general.

This is followed by Fredric Jameson's analysis of the importance of the pastiche for postmodernism. It is somewhat a simplification to say so, but one can equate postmodernism and the pastiche. We can think of the pastiche as the form in which postmodernist thought manifests itself. Jameson asserts that what we call postmodernism is really modernism that assumes the form capitalism takes in advanced industrial societies. Jameson is a prominent Marxist thinker and one of the most important theorists of postmodernism.

Next comes a discussion by Best and Kellner of the term "post" in postmodernism and the notion that postmodernism is a temporal or periodizing term— something that comes after something else, namely, modernism. From here I move to a piece by Jack Solomon on the lack of a core identity in people in postmodern societies, with only roles to play, which raises the question of what identity is and whether people who keep changing their identities actually can be said to have an identity. Solomon also deals with the link between postmodernism, popular culture, and consumer culture. This linkage is discussed by many scholars in this book. Lyotard's selection on eclecticism as a postmodern trope follows and also deals with the role of popular culture in our daily lives: we listen to reggae, eat McDonald's hamburgers, and mix everything up whatever way we want to. It offers an example of the impact of postmodern thought on our lifestyles.

Michel Foucault then discusses the importance of games in societies where illusion is the critical factor. Foucault is also associated with the notion that power ultimately shapes our beliefs. He considers another important matter related to our concerns: how cultures can change radically in a very short period of time. One of the central arguments of the postmodernists is that there has been a radical change in our societies as we've moved from modernism to postmodernism as the core of our belief system.

Jean Baudrillard, one of the most celebrated (in America, at least) postmodernist theorists, then deals with the attempt by postmodernism to salvage some kind of meaningful life from the remnants of modernism and history and the notion that simulations and hyperreality are now more important than reality and the "real" thing. The Norman Denzin selection offers a useful summary of four of the main influences of postmodernism on society and provides an overview of the postmodern movement.

The selection by Nietzsche, written around 1885, provides a seminal statement of the philosophical underpinnings of postmodern thought. He writes about his aversion to "total" views of the world, calling to mind Lyotard's "incredulity toward metanarratives." Nietzsche's notion that we can't know reality but only certain perspectives on reality, and the importance of interpretation, are also central notions in postmodern thought. Linda Hutcheon's interview relates postmodernism to feminism, as does the tenth selection, by the feminist scholar Julia Kristeva, who points out, in her remarkable study of attitudes toward women over history, how sexuality has been absorbed into maternity. She also deals with the attempts many women are making now to find a new way to represent femininity. Her essay combines erudite scholarship and very lyrical passages in which she describes her experience of motherhood.

Among the other selections, we find one by Ferdinand de Saussure, who explains that concepts are defined differentially because of the nature of language. Since concepts have no meaning in themselves but obtain meaning only in terms of the relationships in which they are found, we make sense of concepts by comparing them with other terms—most often their opposites. This is the basis for structuralism, which focuses on the relationship between elements in an entity or structure. Structuralists look for the unconscious codes and myths that, they argue, can be found in these structures and that affect them in profound ways. The French anthropologist Claude Lévi-Strauss is one of the most famous adherents of structuralism.

I also have a selection from Roland Barthes on "the death of the author." Barthes is one of the most influential culture critics of recent years and has written on semiotics, mythology (ideology hidden in popular culture), and numerous other subjects. Barthes argues that the old focus on the author of texts and the neglect of their readers is incorrect.

bell hooks, a well-known African American scholar, deals with the relationship between postmodernism and racism and with the importance of rap music as a means of political expression for black people. Charles Jencks considers postmodern architecture and its relation to democratic, rather than elitist, notions of architecture and design. Jencks is a distinguished architect and one of the most important theorists of postmodernism as it relates to architecture.

I offer a selection by Susan Sontag on the significance of "camp" as a kind of indicator or precursor of postmodernism. Sontag was one of the first American thinkers to recognize the importance of postmodernism. I also offer a typographically interesting selection by Hélène Cixous, a French feminist scholar who is interested in the role language plays in the relationship between men and women. Her selection, with its attack on linguistic oppositions that always privilege the male in male/female relationships, recalls Saussure's notions about difference in language and the notion that concepts don't have meaning in themselves but only as the opposite of other concepts.

Saussure's notions were attacked by Jacques Derrida, who is generally considered one of the most important contemporary philosophers. I have a selection from him on "différance." He is identified with deconstruction and the movement known as poststructuralism, which argues, in essence, that Saussure's ideas about signs are too simplistic. Saussure defines a sign as a combination of a *signifier* (sound/image) and a *signified* (concept). The relationship that exists between the two is always arbitrary, and the combination generates a discrete idea or some kind of meaning.

Derrida and the poststructuralists argue that the signifying process never ends—it is never-ending, as one signifier calls to mind other signifiers and the process continues on and on. Poststructuralists give more importance to the signifier than to the signified and stress that meaning is always unstable. As Derrida has written (1973: 58), "The meaning of meaning is infinite implication, the indefinite referral of signifier to signified. . . . Its force is a certain pure and infinite equivocality which gives signified meaning no respite, no rest. . . . It always signified again and differs." Meaning, Derrida asserts, ultimately comes from the way signifiers relate to one another intertextually—that is, the way texts imitate or are based upon one another, often in rather complicated ways. Signifiers don't generate one simple meaning and stop at that.

There are some fifty selections in this book, covering everything from post-modern theory to the effects of postmodernism on different aspects of our daily life. I deal with some important theoretical statements, but I also show how postmodernism has affected our architecture, therapy, advertising, films, consumer behavior, and many other aspects of our daily lives.

5. What Issues Does Postmodernism Raise?

While there are any number of philosophical and other issues that are found in what might be called the "postmodernism debate," there are two that are of particular interest.

The first issue involves postmodernism's identity: Is postmodernism really a kind of modernism masked in wolf's clothing, so to speak, or does it have its own discrete identity apart from modernism? That is, does postmodernism represent a rupture with modernism, and is postmodernism, as various authors have suggested, a "mutation" and something that is radically different from modernism? Or is it just a new form of modernism that is tied to the development of capitalism?

Fredric Jameson, an influential postmodernist Marxist thinker titled one of his books *Postmodernism, or The Cultural Logic of Late Capitalism*. He argues that postmodernism is *not* a cultural dominant for a new order but represents, instead, a new and "late" stage in the development of capitalism. It is the economic system, capitalism, that pays the piper and calls the so-called postmodernist tune. In this book you will find arguments on both sides of this issue, but I believe that the prevailing opinion among scholars and critics is that postmodernism is something unique and stands apart from modernism.

The second major issue involves the question of whether postmodernism is relativistic. Postmodernists do not accept the old narratives that provided generations of people with notions about truth and how to behave; these notions are found in systematic philosophical systems such as religions and political ideologies. The "perspectivist" point of view, which stems from the philosopher Friedrich Nietzsche's writings, suggests that facts don't exist independent of the perspectives of the people asserting them. All that we can do, Nietzsche tells us, is offer our interpretations of reality, which means the more interpretations we can offer of something, the closer we come to finding out the truth of the matter. But some perspectives, Nietzsche tells us, are better than others, which means that Nietzsche is not a relativist and does not argue that there's no such thing as truth and that anyone's opinion is as good as anyone else's.

As Nietzsche writes in his book *The Will to Power* (1967: 330), "the value of the world lies in our interpretation . . . that every elevation of man brings with it the overcoming of narrower interpretations; that every strengthening and increase of power opens up new perspectives and means believing in new horizons—this idea permeates my writings." Consider, for example, a group of people standing in circle around a statue. Each person sees part of the statue and can describe what he or she sees, but nobody sees the complete statue. So we are always seeing reality from a particular perspective. If we could add up everyone's partial view, we'd get a description of the "real" statue.

Postmodernist thinkers have been influenced by Nietzsche's perspectivism and also his antirationalism. Neil Nehring discusses this antirationalist aspect of Nietzsche's thought in *Popular Music, Gender, and Postmodernism*. He explains that Nietzsche's celebration of Dionysian energies led to his philosophy being seen as radical and that his notion that progress is a mistaken idea appealed to the disenchantment many postmodernist theorists felt with the Enlightenment's faith in reason. Nietzsche's emphasis on exercising power also struck a chord with postmodernist theorists, and with Michel Foucault and his followers in particular (1997: 38).

Nietzsche, then, has played a pivotal role in the development of postmodern thought—both because of his emphasis on irrationality and emotion and because of his perspectivism. This perspectivism, as I pointed out earlier, is not the same thing as relativism. The argument of the perspectivists is that all we can do is try to learn what we can about reality, but that in every case what we know and what we posit as fact is influenced by our perspectives on things and by such considerations as the language we use, where we live, and the time period in which we live. Postmodernist thinkers tend to attack those who espouse all-embracing philosophies and absolutes, suggesting that these philosophers and their ideas are generally only apologists for special interests. Those on the opposite side accuse postmodernists of being nihilists and of not believing in any truths at all.

So the question remains: How can you establish just societies without universally accepted beliefs in such notions as truth, the rule of law, and equality? This question tends to be neglected by many postmodernist thinkers, who focus most of their attention on culture and tend to put social and political matters on the back burner. There is no final answer to this question about postmodernism and relativism; it represents one important aspect of the debate on postmodernism. What we find is that various postmodernist thinkers try to offer convincing arguments to support their position on whether or not postmodernism is relativistic.

Can a Book in the Form of a Pastiche (Or Is It a Pastiche in the Form of a Book?) Have a Meaning to It?

This book is a pastiche, a hodgepodge. In pastiches, the meaning arises out of a kind of gestalt, with the total adding up to more than the individual pieces. Think, for example, of a collage, which is made of scraps of this and that. Each scrap or fragment is relatively insignificant, but they all form an interesting image when assembled together.

If I were a more doctrinaire postmodernist, I could have assembled each selection and commentary on a large card, shuffled my collection of cards, and presented them in the random way they became ordered in my deck of cards. (Each time I shuffled the deck, I'd come up with a different ordering of selections and a different book. Thus, *The Portable Postmodernist* would not be one book but 100,000 or more possible books.) But the logical, rational "modernist" in me prevented me from doing so.

I have suggested that postmodernism and modernism are, like conjoined twins, joined together at the hip. You cannot understand what postmodernism is unless you have some understanding of what modernism is. And you can't understand modernism without understanding premodernism (a term that is actually used), or whatever you want to call the period that preceded modernism.

I might point out that there isn't agreement on how to write the term "postmodernism." Should it be one word—postmodernism—or two words—postmodernism—joined by a hyphen? You will see it spelled both ways. Postmodernists can't agree on very much, as you can see. So in some selections, postmodernism is spelled without a hyphen and in others it is spelled with a hyphen. I have kept the spelling each author used, though in recent years, most people have omitted the hyphen.

I have covered the impact of postmodernism on a number of different fields in this book. I have dealt with architecture, literature, communication theory, politics, pop culture, romantic love, and American culture and society, among other things. For many postmodernist theorists, America is the quintessentially postmodern society. And though we may not recognize it as such and may be unaware of the all-pervasive influence of postmodernism upon us, on both the sociocultural and the personal level, if the postmodernist theorists are correct, we now have what might be called a postmodernist sensibility. And this sensibility has shaped our society, our view of life, and our identities.

If you want to better understand the significance of the modernist and postmodernist split in my psyche (and that of millions of other people in the United States and elsewhere), what makes a postmodern building postmodern, why *Blade Runner* is a postmodernist film, how postmodernism may be affecting your love life, and how punk relates to postmodernism, read on.

Green Marilyn, Andy Warhol. Gift of William C. Seitz and Irma S. Seitz, in Honor of the 50th Anniversary of the National Gallery of Art, Photograph © 2002 Board of Trustees, National Gallery of Art, Washington 1962.

1 **Lyotard on "Incredulity toward Metanarratives"**

Simplifying to the extreme, I define *postmodern* as incredulity toward metanarratives. This incredulity is undoubtedly a product of progress in the sciences: but that progress in turn presupposes it. To the obsolescence of the metanarrative apparatus of legitimation corresponds, most notably, the crisis of metaphysical philosophy and of the university institution which in the past relied on it. The narrative function is losing its functors, its great hero, its great dangers, its great voyages, its great goal.

— JEAN-FRANÇOIS LYOTARD, *The Postmodern Condition: A Report on Knowledge* (Minneapolis: University of Minnesota Press, 1984), xxiv.

What is Metanarrative

This somewhat elliptical statement, in which Lyotard defines postmodernism as involving "incredulity toward metanarratives," is probably one of the most famous definitions of the term ever written. We no longer have faith, Lyotard argues, in the great all-encompassing, wide-ranging supernarratives—the systems of thought (as expounded in religions, political ideologies, and philosophy) that have grounded us in the past. Instead, in a postmodern world, we have many different narratives vying for our attention, which has led to a crisis of legitimation. Who has the answers? Whose beliefs are valid? What's right and wrong?

In a postmodern world, such questions are—or seem to be—left up in the air. Whether postmodernism is as relativistic as many claim is a debatable matter, a matter that is part of the controversy about postmodernism. If you don't accept one "universal" standard, does it mean you have no standards? Kant has a concept, the "categorical imperative," that is relevant here. Kant says if you want to know whether an act is moral, you should be willing to put it to the test—it should be an act that you would be willing to have all humankind do.

But just because you don't believe in the categorical imperative doesn't mean that you don't believe in any imperative. Just because postmodernists don't believe in metanarratives doesn't mean they don't believe in any narratives. But how does one decide which ones are valid?

2 Pastiche

[I]n the dialectical leap from quantity to quality, the explosion of modern literature into a host of distinct private styles and mannerisms has been followed by a linguistic fragmentation of social life itself to the point where the norm itself is eclipsed. . . . Modernist styles thereby become post-modernist codes. And that the stupendous proliferation of social codes today into professional and disciplinary jargons (but also into the badges of affir-mation of ethnic, gender, race, religious, and class-factional adhesion) is also a political phenomenon, the problem of micropolitics sufficiently demon-strates. If the ideas of a ruling class were once the dominant (or hegemonic) ideology of bourgeois society, the advanced capitalist countries today are now a field of stylistic and discursive heterogeneity without a norm. Faceless masters continue to inflect the economic strategies which constrain our existences, but they no longer need to impose their speech (or are henceforth unable to); and the postliteracy of the late capitalist world reflects not only the absence of any great collective project but also the unavailability of the older national language itself.

In this situation parody finds itself without a vocation; it has lived, and that strange new thing pastiche slowly comes to take its place. Pastiche is, like parody, the imitation of a peculiar or unique, idiosyncratic style, the wearing of a linguistic mask, speech in a dead language. But it is a neutral practice of such mimicry, without any of parody's ulterior motives, ampu-tated of the satiric impulse, devoid of laughter and of any conviction that alongside the abnormal tongue you have momentarily borrowed, some healthy linguistic normality still exists. Pastiche is thus blank parody, a statue with blind eyeballs: it is to parody what that other interesting and his-torically original modern thing, the practice of a kind of blank irony, is to what Wayne Booth calls the "stable ironies" of the eighteenth century.

— FREDRIC JAMESON, "Postmodernism, or, The Cultural Logic of
Late Capitalism," *New Left Review,* no. 146 (July–August 1984),
59–92.

This passage from Fredric Jameson's landmark essay on postmodernism offers many of the most important themes in Jameson's thinking about the subject. Modernist styles are absorbed into postmodernism, suggesting that there is not a radical break between modernism and postmodernism. Postmodernism, Jameson argues, is best understood as a stage in the development of late capitalism and thus has an economic and political base. In addition, Jameson asserts that there is a kind of normlessness that exists now in postmodernist societies, with thousands of different social codes and subcultures striving for their place in the sun.

In this chaotic situation, pastiche replaces parody as a dominant force. Pastiche is also neutral—it does not have parody's implicit satirical intent, its sense of humor, or its critical focus. Pastiche, by its very nature, draws upon the past, cannibalizing whatever it can. (You can see this particularly well in architecture, where a postmodernist building may have a number of different architectural styles all mixed together.) Thus, Jameson tells us, the "culture of the simulacrum comes to life," and images now dominate. Many of these themes are repeated in the works of postmodernist theorists to whom you will be introduced in the pages that follow.

A pastiche is, for our purposes, a literary work made up of selections from other works. In the visual arts, pastiches are called collages. When you step back from a collage, you see that the various selections, like tiles in a mosaic, give you an aesthetically interesting image. Like pastiches, collages combine materials from elsewhere—fragments from newspapers, bits of material, advertisements, photographs, and all kinds of other things—to create a complex image. Just as bits and pieces make up a collage, so do our lives, postmodernists argue, reflect this fragmentation that has taken place in the postmodern world.

The Portable Postmodernist is a book of selections from different authors and theorists of postmodernism on various aspects of postmodernism. What emerges is a pastiche . . . a literary work that gives us a picture, so to speak, of what postmodernism is, why it is important, and what its impact has been by using—in the best postmodern tradition—a series of short "takes" from the writings of many different scholars, philosophers, thinkers, speculators, artists, gurus. My task as the assembler of this work is to create a picture, or perhaps an experience, by ordering the fragments in a way that turns postmodernism into something approaching a narrative.

3 The "Post" in Postmodernism

Postmodern discourses thus denote new artistic, cultural, or theoretical perspectives which renounce modern discourses and practices. All of these "post" terms function as sequential markers, designating that which follows and comes after the modern. The discourse of postmodernism thus involves periodizing terms which describe a set of key changes in history, society, culture, and thought. The confusion involved in the discourse of the postmodern results from its usage in different fields and disciplines and the fact that most theorists and commentators on postmodern discourse provide definitions and conceptualizations that are frequently at odds with each other and usually inadequately theorized. Moreover some theorists and commentators use the term postmodernism descriptively, to describe new phenomena, while others use it prescriptively, urging the adoption of new theoretical, cultural, and political discourses and practices.

There is, in fact, an ambiguity inherent in the word "post" which is played out in various postmodern discourses. On the one hand, "post" describes a "not" modern that can be read as an active term of negation which attempts to move beyond the modern era and its theoretical and cultural practices. Thus, postmodern discourses and practices are frequently characterized as anti-modern interventions which explicitly break with modern ideologies, styles, and practices that many postmodernists see as oppressive or exhausted. The prefix "post", in this prescriptive sense, signifies an active rupture (*coupure*) with what preceded it. As we have noted, this rupture can be interpreted positively as a liberation from old constraining and oppressive conditions ... and as an affirmation of new developments, a moving into new terrains, a forging of new discourses and ideas.... Or the new postmodernity can be interpreted negatively as a deplorable regression, a loss of traditional values, certainties, and stabilities ... or as a surrender of those still valuable elements of modernity.... On the other hand, the "post" in postmodern also signifies a dependence on continuity with that which it follows, leading critics to conceptualize the postmodern as merely an intensification of the modern, as a hypermodernity ... a new "face of modernity" ... or a "postmodern" development within modernity.... Yet many postmodern theorists deploy the term—as it was introduced by Toynbee—to characterize a dramatic rupture or break in Western history. The discourses of the postmodern therefore presuppose a sense of an ending, the advent of something new, the demand that we must develop new categories, theories, methods to explore and conceptualize this novum, this novel social and cultural situation. Thus, there is an intrinsic pathos of new which characterizes the discourses of the postmodern and its celebrants tend to position themselves as theoretical and political avant-gardes (just as "modern" theorists did in an earlier era).

We will therefore use the term "postmodernist" to describe the avatars of the postmodern within the fields of philosophy, cultural theory, and social theory. A postmodernist describes and usually champions imputed breaks in knowledge, culture, and society, frequently attacking the modern while identifying with what they tout as new and "radical" postmodern discourses and practices.

— STEVEN BEST and DOUGLAS KELLNER, *Postmodern Theory: Critical Interrogations* (New York: Guilford, 1991), 29–30.

B est and Kellner point out that one problem people have in dealing with postmodernism is that it involves a number of different areas—social theory, politics, and culture—and thus postmodernists often confuse people because what postmodernist theorists and critics write about one field may not seem to apply to another. On the other hand, one can argue that there is a core, a common base of assumptions, found in the various postmodernisms, involving "incredulity toward metanarratives" and a stylistic eclecticism that manifests itself in many different areas of contemporary life.

There is also the semantic confusion attached to the word "post," so that "postmodern" can mean "after" modern, "not" modern, or "going beyond" modern. Thus, some theorists see postmodernism as an intensification or modification of modernism and downplay the so-called break or rupture that other theorists argue exists between postmodernism and modernism.

To further complicate matters, there is some question about what modernism is. I will offer some descriptions of modernism shortly, since it helps to know what modernism is if you want to understand what postmodernism is—and isn't. It is worth keeping in mind the warning Best and Kellner give us—postmodernists are frequently at odds with one another about what postmodernism is, how it affects people, and what its impact on our society, politics, and culture has been.

4　Postmodernism and Pop

In the postmodern worldview, there is no such thing as an essential "me," no centering self-identity, no inborn character. There are only roles, images we take up in imitation of other images. The careers of such postmodern pop celebrities as Madonna, David Bowie, and Michael Jackson are paradigmatic. Madonna began by playing the role of a "punk" rockstar in her "Like a Virgin" phase and then redefined herself in the image of an even more potent TV-age icon, Marilyn Monroe. David Bowie has played every role from Ziggy Stardust to the title role in the film *The Man Who Fell to Earth.* Michael Jackson has gone from Motown to sadomasochistic black leather, allegedly altering his hair, facial features, and skin color in the process.

You can see it all happening every day on MTV, where the fetishized image reaches its pop cultural apotheosis. In an MTV video, the look is every-thing: character, the spirit that lives beneath the skin, is nothing. Images are put on and taken off at will, each new role unencumbered by the need for a coherent plot. . . . For all its ironic mockery of the iconography of mass cul-ture, however, postmodernism has proven to be a profitable ally of corporate America. MTV videos, after all, sell records. . . . Coca-Cola commercials often resemble rock videos, creating a dizzying montage of celebrity and non-celebrity images, that fosters an illusion of intimacy between the ad viewers—who can see themselves in the noncelebrity frames. . . .

I suppose it was inevitable. In a culture devoted to the transformation of products into images, one could hardly expect to see the postmodern flair for image production passed up. Nor has Madison Avenue ignored the distinc-tively narrativeless texture of the postmodern imagination. Traditional com-mercials often set up a narrative situation of some sort, which, though trivial, has a beginning, a middle, and an end—as when Mrs. Olson saves her young neighbors' marriage by introducing them to Folger's Coffee. But in Calvin Klein's postmodern campaign for Obsession perfume, it's virtually impossible to tell just what is going on. A tormented woman seems to be torn between a young boy and an older man—or does the young boy represent a flashback to the older man's youth? Maybe it's her kid brother? Her son? She touches his face for an instant but refuses to be touched and glides away. Tears run down her glacial Art Deco face, but it isn't clear what she's crying about. She speaks a few words, but their meaning is obscure. A surrealistic dream vision rather than a coherent narrative, the Obsession commercial substitutes eccentric imagery for narrative significance. What matters is the "look," the inscrutable aura of postmodern chic.

— JACK SOLOMON, *The Signs of Our Time* (Los Angeles: Jack Tarcher, 1988), 227–29.

Solomon discusses a number of themes that we will find pervading the writings of postmodernists: the relation between postmodernism and images, and the use by advertising agencies of postmodernism in the creation of many of their commercials and advertisements. The modernist perspective on stories—they should have a beginning, middle, and end—has been eclipsed by the postmodern emphasis on look and style. In a world dominated by images, and images of images (so we often have trouble determining what is "real"), our identities become infinitely malleable. We don't seem to have a core to our beings but move from one look to the next with incredible rapidity. In so doing, we may be losing our identities. This notion that we can create and recreate ourselves endlessly suggests that individual human beings are all-important and that we are not affected by society and culture. If this is so, where did we all pick up the postmodern sensibility, and how do we decide which image to try on? The notion of the self-made man and the self-made woman, it has been said, relieves God of a lot of responsibility.

It is interesting to consider the role of MTV as an important example of the postmodern sensibility at work. MTV, we learn, is all based on images and unconcerned with narrative or plot. Maybe one aspect of postmodernism involves the way MTV reflects and affects our lives. Like MTV, our lives in postmodern societies seem to be all images and no plot or narrative line. But how long can images or "attitude" sustain us?

5 ▶ Postmodernism as Eclecticism

Eclecticism is the degree zero of contemporary general culture: one listens to reggae, watches a western, eats McDonald's food for lunch and local cuisine for dinner, wears Paris perfume in Tokyo and "retro" clothes in Hong Kong; knowledge is a matter for TV games. It is easy to find a public for eclectic works. By becoming kitsch, art panders to the confusion which reigns in the "taste" of patrons. Artists, gallery owners, critics and the public wallow together in the "anything goes," and the epoch is one of slackening. But this realism of the "anything goes" is in fact that of money; in the absence of aesthetic criteria, it remains possible and useful to assess the works of art according to the profit they yield. Such realism accommodates all tendencies, just as capital accommodates all "needs," providing that the tendencies and needs have purchasing power. As for taste, there is no need to be delicate when one speculates or entertains oneself.

— JEAN-FRANÇOIS LYOTARD, *The Postmodern Condition: A Report on Knowledge* (Minneapolis: University of Minnesota Press, 1984), 76.

Here, Lyotard suggests that underneath the randomness and chaos of postmodern culture, in a culture in which eclecticism rules, in which anything goes, in which there are no standards as far as taste is concerned, there is actually one unifying factor—money. That raises an interesting question: Is postmodernism one more marketing ploy meant to enlarge markets, put over on us by the ad world? This selection takes up the same theme that Solomon (who was discussed in the previous section) used in his book on semiotics and contemporary culture—namely, that postmodernism, for all its scorn of bourgeois lifestyles and values, is connected to that most bourgeois value of all, a belief in the all-importance of the almighty dollar, or euro, or whatever.

The problem eclecticism poses for us is that it appears (a word chosen with a considerable amount of care) that we become lost in a rapid succession of images as we try on and cast off one identity after another and lose any sense of self we have—assuming that a self involves some kind of coherent sense of one's identity. But that definition may be a modernist one, and the concept of the self may be meaningless in postmodern societies.

6 ▸ Postmodernism, the Loss of the Old Credulities, and Games

Discontinuity—the fact that within the space of a few years a culture sometimes ceases to think as it had been thinking up till then and begins to think other things in a new way—probably begins with an erosion from outside, from that space which is, for thought, on the other side, but in which it has never ceased to think from the very beginning. Ultimately, the problem that presents itself is that of the relations between thought and culture: how is it that thought has a place in the space of the world, that it has its origin here, and that it never ceases, in this place or that, to begin anew? But perhaps it is not yet time to pose this problem; perhaps we should wait until the archaeology of thought has been established more firmly, until it is better able to gauge what it is capable of describing directly and positively, until it has defined the particular systems and internal connections it has to deal with, before attempting to encompass thought and to investigate how it contrives to escape itself. . . .

At the beginning of the seventeenth century, during the period that has been termed, rightly or wrongly, the Baroque, thought ceases to move in the element of resemblance. Similitude is no longer the form of knowledge but rather the occasion of error, the danger to which one exposes oneself when one does not examine the obscure region of confusions. "It is a frequent habit," says Descartes, in the first lines of his *Regulae,* "when we discover several resemblances between two things, to attribute to both equally, even on points in which they are in reality different, that which we have recognized to be true of only one of them." The age of resemblance is drawing to a close. It is leaving nothing behind but its games. Games whose power of enchantment grow out of the new kinship between resemblance and illusion; the chimeras of similitude loom up on all sides, but they are recognized as chimeras; it is the privileged age of *trompe-l'oeil* painting, of the comic illusion, of the play that duplicates itself by representing another play, of the *quid pro quo,* of dreams and visions; it is the age of the deceiving senses; it is the age in which the poetic dimension of language is defined by metaphor, simile, and allegory.

And it was also in the nature of things that the knowledge of the sixteenth century should leave behind it the distorted memory of a muddled and disordered body of learning in which all the things in the world could be linked indiscriminately to men's experiences, traditions, or credulities.

— MICHEL FOUCAULT, *The Order of Things: An Archaeology of the Human Sciences* (New York: Vintage, 1973), 51.

Foucault focuses on one of the more important aspects of postmodernism—the notion that illusion is now dominating our lives, that the age of resemblance has given way to the age of illusion. The kind of painting that fools the eye, that imitates a photograph, is now gaining the upper hand over paintings that rely on resemblance. Foucault's notion that games are the residue of modernist culture is a theme that pervades postmodernist culture. It may be that the postmodernists are playing games with us, that they are having fun at our expense, and their greatest triumph may be that we are taking them seriously. Is postmodernism a big put-on? That's something we must keep in mind. What makes the matter difficult is that the put-on is a characteristic of postmodernism, along with a fascination with images and illusion and an ironic stance, which says, "Believe the opposite of what I say."

Foucault's comment about the power of discontinuity, of how a culture can, in the space of just a few years or so, stop thinking the way it had been thinking and think in a new way, seems to describe what has happened as postmodern thought has, suddenly it seems, replaced modernist thought and given people new ways of thinking about themselves and the world. The old credulities have given way, seemingly out of the blue, to what Lyotard describes as "incredulities."

7 Four Aspects of Postmodernism

The postmodern as postmodernism is four things at the same time. First, it describes a sequence of historical movements from World War II to the present.... Secondly, the postmodern references the multinational forms of late capitalism which have introduced new cultural logics, and new forms of communication and representation into the world economic and cultural systems. Thirdly, it describes a movement in the visual arts, architecture, cinema, popular music, and social theory which goes against the grain of classic realist and modernist formations. Fourthly, it references a form of theorizing and writing about the social which is post-positivist, interpretive, and critical. Postmodern theorizing is preoccupied with the visual society, its representations, cultural logics, and the new types of personal troubles (AIDS, homelessness, drug addiction, family, and public violence) and public problems that define the current usage.... But postmodernism is more than a series of economic formations. The postmodern society, as suggested above, is a cinematic, dramaturgical production. Film and television have transformed American, and perhaps all other, societies touched by the camera, into video, visual cultures. Representations of the real have become stand-ins for actual, lived experience. Three implications follow from the cinematization of contemporary life.

First, reality is a staged, social production. Secondly, the real is now judged against its staged, cinematic-video counterpart. . . . Third, the metaphor of the dramaturgical society . . . or "life as theater" . . . has now become international reality. The theatrical aspects of the dramaturgical metaphor have not "only creeped into everyday life" . . . they have taken it over. Art not only mirrors life, it structures it and reproduces it. The postmodern society is a dramaturgical society.

Accordingly, the postmodern scene is a series of cultural formations which impinge upon, shape, and define contemporary human group life. These formations are anchored in a series of institutional sites, including the mass media, the economy, and the polity, the academy and popular culture. In these sites interacting individuals come in contact with postmodernism, which, like the air we breathe, is everywhere around us: in the omnipresent camera where lives and money exchange hands; in the sprawling urban shopping malls; in films like *Blue Velvet;* in the evening televised news; in soap operas and situation comedies; in the doctor's office and the police station; at the computer terminal.

— NORMAN K. DENZIN, *Images of Postmodern Society: Social Theory and Contemporary Cinema* (Thousand Oaks, Calif.: Sage, 1991), ix–x.

Now for a bit of historical perspective and some elaboration on the general theme of what postmodernism is. Denzin points out that postmodernism is a periodization—it deals with culture after World War II and is connected to economic and aesthetic matters. (Some people define the "post" as meaning "going beyond" and not just "coming after.") It repudiates modernism, which refers to the period from the turn of the century to World War II, and it is very much involved with visual culture, images, the media, and the notion that "representations of the real" have become increasingly important. More important, some would say, than reality. That may be why people often are more interested in watching events on television than actually seeing them in the flesh. We have become habituated to the mass-mediated experience, to the zooms and cutting of television, and reality now pales in comparison.

Denzin suggests that our culture has become so dominated by the postmodern aesthetic and the postmodern sensibility that we cannot escape it. He also suggests that postmodernism turns the old notion that "life imitates art" on its head. The mimetic theory of art says that "art imitates life." Denzin argues that in postmodern, dramaturgical societies, where we are always playing roles and changing roles, life now imitates art. Life has become a kind of theater in which we are always taking on new roles (that is, identities) and casting them off, the way Hollywood film actors do when they take on new roles in new films, except that, generally speaking, we play out our roles in malls and shopping centers.

8 Nietzsche and Postmodernism

470. (1885–1886)

Profound aversion to reposing once and for all in any one total view of the world. Fascination of the opposing point of view: refusal to be deprived of the stimulus of the enigmatic.

481. (1883-1888)

Against positivism, which halts at phenomena—There are only *facts.*—I would say: No, facts is precisely what there is not, only interpretations. We cannot establish any fact "in itself": perhaps it is folly to want to do such a thing.

"Everything is subjective," you say; but even this is interpretation invented and projected behind what there is.—Finally, is it necessary to posit an interpreter behind the interpretation? Even this is invention, hypothesis.

In so far as the word "knowledge" has any meaning, the world is knowable; but it is *interpretable* otherwise, it has no meaning behind it, but countless meanings.—"Perspectivism."

It is our needs that interpret the world; our drives and their For and Against. Every drive is a lust to rule; each one has its perspective that it would to compel all the other drives to accept as a norm.

600. (1885–1886)

No limit to the ways in which the world can be interpreted; every interpretation as symptom of growth or of decline.

Inertia needs unity (monism); plurality of interpretations a sign of strength. Not to desire to deprive the world of its disturbing and enigmatic character!

604. (1885–1886)

"Interpretation," the introduction of meaning—not "explanation" (in most cases a new interpretation over an old interpretation that has become incomprehensible, that is now itself only a sign). There are no facts, everything is in flux, incomprehensible, elusive; what is relatively most enduring is—our opinions.

— FRIEDRICH NIETZSCHE, *The Will to Power,* trans. R. Hollingdale and W. Kaufmann (New York: Random House, 1987).

These passages from Nietzsche's *Will to Power* show that a number of the themes associated with postmodernism were discussed by Nietzsche as early as 1883. We see, for example, that he distrusts "total" views of the world, just as contemporary postmodernists do. When Lyotard writes about the "incredulity toward metanarratives" that we find in postmodern thought, he is essentially updating Nietzsche.

In the same way, the postmodern aversion to facts and the idea of absolute truths was elaborated by Nietzsche more than a hundred years ago. He emphasizes, like the postmodernists who followed him, that we can't "know" facts and reality, but only interpret them. There are, he tells us, "countless meanings" to the world, which suggests his position—perspectivism.

What fuels our battles over truth and reality and facts is, as Nietzsche puts it, "a kind of lust to rule." We want everyone else to accept our perspective on things as the true perspective. There is, then, behind assertions that philosophers make about reality a psychological need to triumph over others, or what Nietzsche describes as a will to power.

9 Theorizing Feminism and Postmodernity: A Conversation with Linda Hutcheon (1997)

(Kathleen O'Grady) I noted with great interest that your definition of postmodernism (in *The Politics of Postmodernism*) states that this movement, particularly its attention to difference and marginality, has been significantly shaped by feminism. Most commentators—those compiling the anthologies and encyclopedias—have stated the opposite: that feminism is the direct result of a burgeoning postmodernism. This may seem a trivial observation—the beginnings of a "chicken and egg" argument—but it may also be indicative of the proclivity of academic texts to consign feminist writers to the sidelines, the happy cheerleaders of the postmodern movement.

(Linda Hutcheon) My sense has always been that there were certain important social movements in the 1960s (and before) that made the postmodern possible: the women's movement (though, of course, the movement existed much earlier, but this wave of it in the 1960s was crucial) and, in North America, the civil rights movement. Suddenly gender and racial differences were on the table for discussion. Once that happened, "difference" became the focus of much thinking—from newer issues of sexual choice and postcolonial history to more familiar ones such as religion and class. I think feminisms (in the plural) were important for articulating early on the variety of political positions possible within the umbrella term of gender— from liberal humanist to cultural materialist. Feminist discussions "complex-ified" questions of identity and difference almost from the start, and raised those upsetting (but, of course, productive) issues of social and cultural marginality.

(Kathleen O'Grady) Why have so many feminist artists and theorists resisted the lure of postmodernism?

(Linda Hutcheon) In part, it has been because the early constructions of the postmodern were resolutely male (and that's one of the reasons I chose to write on the subject): male writers, artists and theorists were for a long time in the foreground. Sometimes this was a real blind-spot; sometimes it was what we might call a form of gender-caution: people were afraid, because of that resistance of feminists, to label women writers or theorists as postmodern. This was, in part, because, women were indeed resisting such labeling, sometimes out of a worry that the political agenda of their feminisms would be subsumed under the "apolitical" aestheticizing label of postmodernism. But it depends on whose definition of the postmodern we are talking about. I happen to think that postmodernism is political, but not in a way that is of much use, in the long run, to feminisms: it does challenge dominant discourses (usually through self-consciousness and parody), but it also re-instates those very discourses in the act of challenging them. To put it another way, postmodernism does deconstruct, but doesn't really reconstruct. No feminist is happy with that kind of potential quietism, even if she (or he) approves of the deconstructing impulse: you simply can't stop there.

— LINDA HUTCHEON, "Theorizing Feminism and Postmodernity," 1997, www.english.ucsb.edu/faculty/ayliu/research/ grady-hutcheon.html [accessed March 15, 2002].

Linda Hutcheon, a Canadian feminist critic, makes an interesting point here—that postmodernism has been profoundly affected by the development of feminist thought. This is the opposite of what most commentators have argued, namely, that postmodernism more or less "liberated" feminism and carried it forward. Hutcheon argues that the women's movement and the civil rights movement made postmodernism possible. Once gender and race became important topics of social and political concern, the matter of difference (and its opposite, similarity) became important, and there was an opening for postmodern thought.

Curiously, though, many feminists have resisted identifying themselves with postmodernism. This happened, in part, because most of the theorists and spokespersons for postmodernism were male and also because many feminists wanted to avoid losing their political focus and being caught up in aesthetic debates.

Hutcheon offers a critique of one limitation of postmodernism: it deconstructs, but it does not reconstruct, which means it is essentially quietistic, and feminist thinkers and writers don't want to accept this position. Postmodernism may challenge dominant discourses (often through parody), but it also reinstates them in the process of challenging them, she argues, so its critique is not as powerful as it might be.

10 Julia Kristeva's "Stabat Mater"

If it is not possible to say of a *woman* what she is (without running the risk of abolishing her difference), would it perhaps be different concerning the *mother,* since it is the only function of the "other sex" to which we can definitely attribute existence? And yet, there too, we are caught in a paradox. First, we live in a civilization where the *consecrated* (religious or secular) representation of femininity is absorbed by motherhood. If, however, one looks at it more closely, this motherhood is the *fantasy* that is nurtured by the adult, man or woman, of a lost territory; what is more, it involves less an idealized archaic mother than the idealization of the *relationship* that binds us to her, one that cannot be localized—an idealization of primary narcissism. Now, when feminism demands a new representation of femininity, it seems to identify motherhood with that idealized misconception and, because it rejects the image and its misuse, feminism circumvents the real experience that fantasy overshadows. The result?—a negation or rejection of motherhood by some avant-garde feminist groups. Or else an acceptance—conscious or not—of its traditional representations by the great mass of people, women and men.

Christianity is doubtless the most refined symbolic construct in which femininity, to the extent that it transpires through it—and it does so incessantly—is focused on *Maternality.* Let us call "maternal" the ambivalent principle that is bound to the species, on the one hand, and on the other stems from an identity catastrophe that causes the Name to topple over into the unnamable that one images as femininity, nonlanguage, or body. Thus Christ, the Son of man, when all is said and done, is "human" only through his mother— as if Christly or Christian humanism could only be a maternalism (that is, besides, what some secularizing trends within its orbit do not cease claiming in their esotericism). . . .

This resorption of femininity within the Maternal is specific to many civilizations, but Christianity, in its own fashion, brings it to its peak. Could it be that such a reduction represents no more than a masculine appropriation of the Maternal, which, in line with our hypothesis, is only a fantasy masking primary narcissism? Or else, might one detect in it, in other respects, the workings of enigmatic sublimation? These are perhaps the workings of masculine sublimation, a sublimation just the same, if it be true that for Freud picturing DaVinci, and even for DaVinci himself, the taming of that economy (of the Maternal or of primary narcissism) is a requirement for artistic, literary, or painterly accomplishment?

— JULIA KRISTEVA, "Stabat Mater," in *The Kristeva Reader,* ed. Julia
   Kristeva and Toril Moi (New York: Columbia University Press, 1986),
   160–61.

Julia Kristeva is a professor at the University of Paris and is known for her work on literary theory, psychoanalytic thought, and feminist philosophy. In "Stabat Mater," Kristeva does two things. First, she deals with the way philosophers and theologians—mostly male—have absorbed femininity into motherhood. She offers a historical overview of the way the Virgin Mary has been seen and interpreted over time. Second, she provides, in bold type, her reactions to her own experiences of being a mother. So we have a kind of pastiche in which philosophical discourse is set off by sections of an autobiographical nature. Thus, "Stabat Mater" is something of a hybrid. One problem with this reduction of the feminine into the maternal is that it is unsatisfactory for women—it narrows our sense of what a woman is and tends to define her, simplistically, as a being whose primary purpose is motherhood. For women, Kristeva suggests, this is unacceptable.

Finally, to give you an idea of what her parallel autobiographical text is like, let me quote a bit of the first of her autobiographical segments:

FLASH—instant of time or of dream without time; inordinately swollen atoms of a bond, a vision, a shiver, a yet formless, unnamable embryo. Epiphanies. Photos of what is not yet visible and that language necessarily skims over from afar, allusively. (1986, 160–161)

We find in these sections a lyrical and poetic sensibility that counters the highly analytical and philosophically complex analysis she offers of the Virgin Mary as she has been seen through history.

11 Postmodernism and Nihilism

Post-modernity is neither optimistic nor pessimistic. It is a game with the vestiges of what has been destroyed. This is why we are "post"—history has stopped, one is in a kind of post-history which is without meaning. One would not be able to find any meaning in it. So, we must move in it, as though it were a kind of circular gravity. We can no longer be said to progress. So it is a "moving" situation. But it is not at all unfortunate. I have the impression with post-modernism that there is an attempt to rediscover a certain pleasure in the irony of things, in the game of things. Right now one can tumble into total — the definitions, everything, it's all been done. What can one do? what can one become? And post-modernity is the attempt—perhaps it's desperate, I don't know—to reach a point where one can live with what is left. It is more a survival amongst the remnants than anything else.

— JEAN BAUDRILLARD, "On Nihilism," *On the Beach* 6 (spring 1984): 38–39.

Jean Baudrillard takes a historical approach to postmodernism here and sees postmodernism as an attempt to salvage some kind of tolerable existence out of the remnants of modernism and history. One of the great metanarratives that sustained us—the idea of progress—has been tossed, he suggests, onto the ash heap of history. We've gone as far as we can go, Baudrillard asserts, and history as we know it has come to an end. Postmodernism represents, then, the "real" game of *Survivor* in a world where everything has, so it seems, been emptied of meaning. Baudrillard's ideas may help explain why *Survivor* and other reality shows on television have been such big hits—we all recognize, subconsciously, that the roles of the characters in these shows are the roles we are forced to take in the new postmodern era, so there is incredible resonance in audiences with these programs. Isn't there something odd about the notion of having reality programming on television? Not if you're living in a postmodern world, one might answer. But would this answer be correct? In a postmodern world such as that described by Baudrillard, would that matter?

12 Postmodernism and Hyperreality

It is reality itself that is hyperrealist. Surrealism's secret already was that the most banal reality could become surreal, but only in certain privileged moments that are still nevertheless connected with art and the imaginary. Today it is quotidian reality in its entirety—political, social, historical and economic—that from now on incorporates the simulating dimension of hyper-realism. We live everywhere already in an "aesthetic" hallucination of reality."

— JEAN BAUDRILLARD, *Simulations* (New York: Semiotext(e),1983), 148.

ere Baudrillard develops one of his most important themes—that reality has been replaced by hyperreality and that the image has become more important than the thing captured by the image. Our quotidian, or everyday, lives are now dominated by simulations, and we live in a world of images, a kind of hallucination in which the images and simulations that pervade our lives have usurped reality.

In an earlier selection, by Jack Solomon, we came across the notion that images have become dominant in our postmodern society—the images of ourselves we create and the images that bombard us on television, in newspapers and magazines, on billboards and buses, everywhere we turn.

13 ▸ Postmodern Art, Literature, and Rules

A postmodern artist or writer is in the position of a philosopher: the text he writes, the work he produces are not in principle governed by preestablished rules and they cannot be judged according to a determining judgment, by applying familiar categories to the text or to the work. Those rules and categories are what the work of art itself is looking for. The artist and the writer, then, are working without rules in order to formulate the rules of what *will have been done.* Hence the fact that work and text have the character of an *event;* hence also, they always come too late for their author, or, what amounts to the same thing, their being put into work, their realization (*mise en oeuvre*) always begin too soon. *Post modern* would have to be understood according to the paradox of the future: (*post*) anterior (*modo*).

— JEAN-FRANÇOIS LYOTARD, *The Postmodern Condition: A Report on Knowledge* (Minneapolis: University of Minnesota Press, 1984),81.

In a world where metanarratives are greeted with incredulity, how does on make sense of a work of postmodern art? That is a dilemma that we all face and that we "solve," if that is the correct term, by recognizing that our task, in dealing with postmodern works or texts, is to formulate the rules by which works are to be understood and judged as we go along. The preestablished rules Lyotard mentions are those that we learned from reading modernist works, but in a post-modernist world, the old rules don't apply. It is worth considering what modernism is and how it related to postmodernism.

This subject is dealt with in the next reading and several others, since you need to understand what modernism is to understand what it isn't—that is, post-modernism. As I point out in this book, and a number of the authors quoted here argue, there is some question about how separated and individuated postmodernism is from modernism; some theorists argue that what we call postmodernism is really only a different stage in the development of modernism.

14 ▶ The Death of the Author

Recent research ... has demonstrated the constitutively ambiguous nature of Greek tragedy, its texts being woven from words with double meanings that each character understands unilaterally (this perpetual misunderstanding is exactly the "tragic"); there is however, someone who understands each word in its duplicity and who, in addition, hears the very deafness of the characters speaking in front of him—this someone being precisely the reader (or here, the listener). Thus is revealed the total existence of writing: a text is made of multiple writings, drawn from many cultures and entering into mutual relations of dialogue, parody, contestation, but there is one place where this multiplicity is focused and that place is the reader, not, as was hitherto said, the author. The reader is the space on which all the quotations that make up a writing are inscribed without any of them being lost; a text's unity lies not in its origin but in its destination. Yet this destination cannot any longer be personal: the reader is without history, biography, psychology; he is simply that *someone* who holds together in a single field all the traces by which the written text is constituted. Which is why it is derisory to condemn the new writing in the name of a humanism hypocritically turned champion of the reader's rights. Classic criticism has never paid any attention to the reader; for it the writer is the only person in literature. We are now beginning to let ourselves be fooled no longer by the arrogant antiphrastical recriminations of good society in favour of the very thing it sets aside, ignores, smothers, or destroys; we know that to give writing its future, it is necessary to overthrow the myth: the birth of the reader must be at the cost of the death of the Author.

— ROLAND BARTHES, "The Death of the Author," in *Image—Music—Text,* trans. Stephen Heath (New York: Hill & Wang, 1977), 148.

Roland Barthes argues in this essay that the way critics have tended to focus all their attention on writers and neglect readers is no longer tenable. It is the reader, Barthes reminds us, who understands the ambiguity and duplicity of the language found in literary texts—and by extension, we can add, all kinds of mass-mediated texts. Barthes also locates texts in the culture, in general, in contrast to those who tend to argue that a text is a highly individual, personal statement. Texts, Barthes points out, draw upon the "multiple writings" that are part of the culture, in general, and it is the reader who interprets texts on the basis of personal experience, education, and cultural memory.

In the best postmodern tradition, Barthes breaks down the separation between author and reader, between a text and the social and cultural milieu in which it is found. Texts may be thought of as individual enunciations or performances, but these performances by themselves are inert—they require an audience that can receive them and make sense of them. Books need readers, and films and television shows need people to see them. So in a postmodern dedifferentiated world, writer and reader are now linked together and recognize that each needs the other.

15 Modernist and Postmodernist Creative Works

As with the pairing of modernity-postmodernity, we are again faced with a range of meanings. Common to them all is the centrality of culture. In the most restricted sense, modernism points to the styles we associate with the artistic movements which originated around the turn of the century and which have dominated the various arts until recently. Figures frequently cited are: Joyce, Yeats, Gide, Proust, Rilke, Kafka, Mann, Musil, Lawrence and Faulkner in literature; Rilke, Pound, Eliot, Lorca, Valéry in poetry; Strindberg and Pirandello in drama; Matisse, Picasso, Braque, Cézanne and the Futurist, Expressionist, Dada and Surrealist movements in painting; Stravinsky, Schoenberg and Berg in music. . . . There is a good deal of debate about how far back into the nineteenth century modernism should be taken (some would want to go back to the bohemian avant-garde of the 1830s). The basic features of modernism can be summarized as: an aesthetic self-consciousness and reflexiveness; a rejection of narrative structure in favour of simultaneity and montage; an exploration of the paradoxical, ambiguous and uncertain open-ended nature or reality; and a rejection of the notion of an integrated personality in favour of an emphasis upon the de-structured, de-humanized subject. . . . The problem with the term [postmodernism] . . . revolves around the question of when does a term defined oppositionally to, and feeding off, an established term start to signify something substantially different?

— MIKE FEATHERSTONE, *Consumer Culture and Postmodernism.*
(London: Sage, 1991), 7.

Featherstone provides a valuable service for us—he offers an expanded list (the list is a postmodernist trope) of the names of some of the most celebrated modernist poets, dramatists, artists, writers, composers, and others involved in the creative world and mentions some of the most important themes connected with modernist works in different areas—aesthetic self-consciousness, a rejection of the traditional narrative structure, a fascination with paradox, and a focus upon a certain kind of personality. Earlier, we read that postmodernists also reject the traditional narrative structure, but the postmodernist rejection of narrative structure is different from the modernist one. The modernists stressed simultaneity and montage; the postmodernists are unconcerned with narrative conventions and focus upon images and style.

Some of these characteristics of modernism, such as the use of montage, seem very close to postmodernist aesthetic practices. It may be that there are large areas of overlap, but at the extremes the two movements are considerably different. Some theorists argue that what we call postmodernism is really just a new kind of modernism and that the so-called debate over modernism and postmodernist is ill-conceived. Postmodernism, for these theorists, is really modernism. One interesting aspect of the whole postmodernism debate is that while postmodernism may have "incredulity toward metanarratives" and be characterized by irony and game playing, books by postmodernists and postmodernism scholars generally use conventional tools of grammar, reasoned arguments, logic, evidence, and other "modernist" means of communication and argumentation.

Saussure on Concepts Being Purely Differential

Language is a system of interdependent terms in which the value of each term results solely from the simultaneous presence of the others....

It is understood that ... concepts are purely differential and defined not by their positive content but negatively by their relations with the other terms of the system. Their most precise characteristic is in being what the others are not.... Signs function, then, not through their intrinsic value but through their relative position.

— FERDINAND DE SAUSSURE, *Course in General Linguistics,* trans. Wade Baskin (New York: McGraw-Hill, 1966), 117–18.

This passage is probably one of the most important statements in the field of semiotics that has ever been written. "In language there are only differences," Saussure asserts elsewhere, and later "the entire mechanism of language ... is based on oppositions." Another way he puts this is, "The whole has value only through its parts, and the parts have value by virtue of their place in the whole. That is why the syntagmatic [sequential] relation of the part to the whole is just as important as the relation of the parts to each other" (1966: 128). What Saussure points out is that concepts—such as postmodernism—don't have any meaning in themselves; their meaning stems from being "what others are not." That is why you will find scholars always contrasting postmodernism with modernism. Postmodernism is, like the uncola, unmodernism, nonmodernism, antimodernism, different from modernism. This means you cannot understand what postmodernism is unless you understand what modernism is, which is why I have selected some passages that deal with the two movements.

It is relations that generate meaning—relations of words in a sentence, relations of concepts in a philosophical dispute. In all cases it is the relationships among the words that generate meaning.

Saussure's book has revolutionized Western thought, for it helps explain how concepts generate meaning and, by implication, how people, institutions, and countries gain an identity. It is all in the differences. Let me suggest how Saussure's notion that concepts are defined differentially works out when it comes to national identity by suggesting that America has frequently defined itself (whether correctly or not is another question) as the un-European country.

Just as Seven-Up has defined itself as the "uncola," we Americans have defined ourselves as the "un-Europeans." Let me offer a set of paired oppositions that reflect how Americans have seen themselves for the past hundred years or so relative to Europe (and perhaps one could add other countries as well). I'm not arguing that our view of ourselves is correct, by any means, but that we have defined ourselves, as we must, by being what others are not. Others, of course, define themselves by being what we are not.

Nature	Culture
America	Europe
Forests	Cathedrals
Cowboy	Cavalier
Frontier	Institutions (church, nobility)
Natural law	Custom
Freedom	Despotism
Innocence	Guilt
Hope	Memory
Willpower	Class conflict
Individualism	Conformity
Agrarianism	Industrialism
Clean living	Sensuality
Achievement	Ascription
Action	Theory
Equality	Hierarchy
Classless society	Class-bound society
Natural foods	Gourmet cooking
The sacred	The profane

Emerson's poem "America, My Country" reflects this polarity and the notion that Americans are different; it also explicitly contrasts America with Europe. Emerson writes that we are a "land without history," a land without kings and cathedrals. Ironically, our universities probably employ half the historians alive, but many of them are there primarily to study other societies, which have a great deal of history. We forge our identities, it would seem, out of a delicate balance between our sense that we are different from others and our behavior, which, in many cases and in many respects (to the extent that it is affected by universal myths), is like that of everyone else or, at least, of large numbers of people.

It is this notion of concepts having meaning by being what others are not that explains why postmodernists feel they must deal with their differences with modernism and rejection of it in order to explain what postmodernism is. Modernism has a credulity toward metanarratives, and postmodernism is characterized by an incredulity toward them. That is one of the fundamental differences between the two, but, as we have seen, there are many others.

17 Derrida on Différance

Why traces? And by what right do we reintroduce grammatics at the moment when we seem to have neutralized every substance, be it phonic, graphic, or otherwise? Of course it is not a question of resorting to the same concept of writing and of simply inverting the dissymmetry that now has become problematical. It is a question, rather, of producing a new concept of writing. This concept can be called *gram* or *différance.* The play of differences supposes, in effect, syntheses and referrals which forbid at any moment, or in any sense, that a simple element be *present* in and of itself, referring only to itself. Whether in the order of spoken or written discourse, no element can function as a sign without referring to another element which itself is not simply present. This interweaving results in each "element"— phoneme or grapheme—being constituted on the basis of the trace within it of the other elements of the chain or system. This interweaving, this textile, is the *text* produced only in the transformation of another text. Nothing, neither among the elements nor within the system, is anywhere ever simply present or absent. There are only, everywhere, differences and traces of traces. The gram, then, is the most general concept of semiology—which thus becomes grammatology—and it covers not only the field of writing in the restricted sense, but also the field of linguistics. The advantage of this concept—provided that it be surrounded by a certain interpretive context, for no more than any other conceptual element it does not signify, or suffice, by itself—is that in principle it neutralizes the phonologistic propensity of the "sign," and *in fact counterbalances* it liberating the entire scientific field of the "graphic substance" (history and systems of writing beyond the bounds of the West) whose interest is not minimal, but which so far has been left in the shadow of neglect.

The gram as *différance,* then, is a structure and a movement no longer conceivable on the basis of the opposition presence/absence. *Différance* is the systematic play of differences, of the traces of differences, of the *spacing* by means of which elements are related to each other.

— JACQUES DERRIDA, *Positions,* trans. Alan Bass (Chicago: University of Chicago Press, 1981), 26–27.

Jacques Derrida is considered to be one of the most important contemporary philosophers. His work, as the material cited above demonstrates, is not easy to follow. That may explain why something like four hundred books have been written about his ideas. He is associated with deconstruction, which offers a radical critique of traditional philosophy and which argues that all texts ultimately undermine their claim to have a fixed meaning and that meaning is always unstable, because of the nature of language.

In this selection, Derrida offers what he describes as a "new concept of writing," which he calls a *gram* or *différance*. The *gram*, then, is instrumental in his theory of grammatology. We can find a vague linkage to Saussure in this passage in which Derrida suggests that nothing is ever present or absent in a text. This recalls Saussure's notion that "concepts are purely differential and defined not by their positive content but negatively by their relations with the other terms of the system" (1966: 117), that meaning stems from relationships, and that nothing has meaning in itself. But Derrida, in various works, attacks the binary thinking that follows from Saussure's work, so Derrida's relation to Saussure is quite complicated. Derrida is, in fact, associated with a movement called poststructuralism, which attempted to move beyond what it thought were the inadequacies of Saussure and the structuralist movement, which was based on his ideas.

For Derrida, texts are always produced by transforming other texts, and everything is based on differences and traces of traces—that is *grams*, a central concept in his thought. Signs, then, are not static but always in play.

Painting

Does the work combine naked figures and old advertising characters in a cryptic, arbitrary manner? Is it painted on broken china? Does the gallery owner call it neo-anything? Is it a photocopy? Do you look at it and say "My 23-year-old could do that?"

Literature

Does the text contain shopping lists, menus, and/or recipes? Does it contain a novel within a novel that has the same title as the novel? Does the cover feature a bunch of little geometric shapes and a quote from Robert Coover? Does it remind you of Céline, if Céline had drunk a lot of Tab? Is it easy to hate?

Movies

Does it remind you of an old movie, except it's set in a post-apocalyptic wasteland? Does it remind you of an old TV show, only it's insincere and has better production values and is longer?

Theater and Performance Art

Are there video monitors, working or not, onstage? Does it seem like a parody of something, only without jokes? Have any of the performers been signed for Susan Seidelman's next film? Is it easier than old-fashioned performance art to like, but just as easy to fall asleep during?

> — BRUCE HANDY, "A *Spy* Guide to Post-modern Everything," quoted in *Utne Reader,* July/August 1989, 61.

This insouciant selection from a *Spy* magazine article on postmodernism gives some of the more common attributes of postmodernism as it is reflected in various media and arts. The article claims that the term was coined in 1949 by J. Hudnut in the book *Architecture and the Spirit of Man*. *Spy* magazine's tone and style also have a touch of the postmodern sensibility. If you don't know who Céline or Robert Coover or Susan Seidelman is, you are lost. So the article's tone suggests it is writing to hip people who already are familiar with many important postmodern artists and writers.

Rather than just talking about the difference between modernism and postmodernism in the arts, I will show it in the next two readings. I have selected two passages from classic works—one from Thomas Pynchon's *Crying of Lot 49*, a postmodern novel, and the other from Robert Musil's *Man without Qualities*, a modernist one.

One summer afternoon Mrs. Oedipa Maas came home from a Tupperware party whose hostess had put perhaps too much kirsch in the fondue to find that she, Oedipa, had been named executor, or she supposed executrix, of the estate of one Pierce Inverarity, a California real estate mogul who had once lost two million dollars in his spare time but still had assets numerous and tangled enough to make the job of sorting it all out more than honorary. Oedipa stood in the living room, stared at by the greenish dead eye of the TV tube, spoke the name of God, tried to feel as drunk as possible. But this did not work. She thought of a hotel room in Mazatlan whose door had just been slammed, it seems forever, waking up two hundred birds down in the lobby; a sunrise over the library slope at Cornell University that nobody out on it had seen because the slope faces west; a dry, disconsolate tune from the fourth movement of the Bartok Concerto for Orchestra; a whitewashed bust of Jay Gould that Pierce kept over the bed on a shelf so narrow for it she'd always had the hovering fear it would someday topple on them. Was that how he'd died, she wondered, among dreams, crushed by the only ikon in his house? That only made her laugh out loud and helpless: You're so sick, Oedipa, she told herself, or the room, which knew.

The letter was from the law firm of Warpe, Wistfull, Kubitschek and McMingus, of Los Angeles, and signed by somebody named Metzger. It said Pierce had died back in the spring, and they'd only just now found the will. Metzger was to act as co-executor. . . . Through the rest of the afternoon, through her trip to the market in downtown Kinneret-Among-The-Pines to buy ricotta and listen to the Muzak (today she came through the bead-curtained entrance around bar 4 of the Fort Wayne Settecento Ensemble's variorum recording of the Vivaldi Kazoo Concerto, Boyd Beaver, soloist); then through the sunned gathering of her marjoram and sweet basil from the hero garden, reading of book reviews in the latest *Scientific American*, into the layering of a lasagna, garlicking of a bread, tearing up of romaine leaves, eventually, then on, into the mixing of the twilight's whisky sours against the arrival of her husband, Wendell ("Mucho") Maas from work. . . . It took her till the middle of Huntley and Brinkley to remember that last year at three or so one morning there had come this long-distance call, from where she would never know (unless now he'd left a diary) by a voice beginning in heavy Slavic tones as second secretary at the Transylvanian Consulate, looking for an escaped bat; modulated to comic-Negro, then on into hostile Pachuco dialect, full of chingas and maricones; then a Gestapo officer asking her in shrieks did she have relatives in Germany and finally his Lamont Cranston voice, the one he'd talked in all the way down to Mazatlan.

— THOMAS PYNCHON, *The Crying of Lot 49* (New York: Bantam, 1967), 1–2.

This is most of the first two paragraphs of Thomas Pynchon's book *The Crying of Lot 49*, a postmodern novel and, in my opinion, a postmodern classic. It is a classic because of the way that Pynchon infuses his novel with themes and characters that reflect, most accurately, the postmodern sensibility. In this novel, it turns out—or so it seems—that there is a parallel post office system working in America that very few people know about. Thus, the opposition between the official post office and a subversive one is collapsed. What is most important about this selection are the quality of the prose; Pynchon's intertextual references to popular culture, which he merges with everyday life (Lamont Cranston was the character known as "the Shadow" in old radio serials); his satire on American life; his use of lists; his humor; and his crazy characters with bizarre names and mixed-up identities—all literary devices used by postmodernist writers.

The novel starts with a common American experience of the fifties (and later), a Tupperware party, then moves on to a quick succession of fantastic images taking place in Mazatlan, at Cornell University, and in Pierce Inverarity's bedroom. Then Pynchon mentions various recondite musical pieces, describes his heroine making dinner, and ends with a bizarre phone call in which a person has taken on a number of different personas: Transylvanian second secretary, comic Negro, hostile Mexican, Gestapo officer, and finally Lamont Cranston, "the Shadow." This selection is short, but it is a very dense bit of writing, with allusions to all kinds of different aspects of American, and in this case southern Californian, culture.

At this moment he wished to be a man without qualities. But this is probably not so very different from what other people sometimes feel too. After all, by the time they have reached he middle of their life's journey few people remember how they have managed to arrive at themselves, at their amusements, their point of view, their wife, character, occupation and successes, but they cannot help feeling that not much is likely to change any more. It might even be asserted that they have been cheated, for one can nowhere discover any sufficient reason for everything's having come about as it has. It might just as well have turned out differently. The events of people's lives have, after all, only to the least degree originated in them, having generally depended on all sorts of circumstances such as the moods, the life or death of quite different people, and have, as it were, only at the given point of time come hurrying towards them. For in youth life still lies before them as an inexhaustible morning, spread out all round them full of everything and nothing; and yet when noon comes there is all at once something there that may justly claim to be their life now, which is, all in all, just as surprising as if one day suddenly there were a man sitting there before one, with whom one had been corresponding for twenty years without knowing him, and all the time imagining him quite different. But what is still much queerer is that most people do not notice this at all; they adopt the man who has come to stay with them, whose life has merged with their own lives and whose experiences now seem to them the expression of their own qualities, his destiny their own merit or misfortune. Something has had its way with them like a fly-paper with a fly; it has caught them fast, here catching a little hair, there hampering their movements, and has gradually enveloped them, until they lie buried under a thick coating that has only the remotest resemblance to their original shape. And then they only dimly remember their youth when there was something like a force of resistance in them—this other force that tugs and whirrs and does not want to linger anywhere, releasing a storm of aimless attempts at flight. Youth's scorn and its revolt against the established order, youth's readiness for everything that is heroic, whether it is self-sacrifice or crime, its fiery seriousness and its unsteadiness—all this is nothing but its fluttering attempts to fly. Fundamentally it merely means that nothing of all that a young man undertakes appears to be the result of an unequivocal inner necessity, even if it expresses itself in such a manner as to suggest that everything he happens to dash at is exceedingly urgent and necessary.

— ROBERT MUSIL, *The Man without Qualities* (New York: Capricorn, 1965), 151–52.

otice the difference between the selections by Pynchon and Musil. It is difficult to deal with entire novels or literary works in short selections, but you still can see that a much different mentality is at work in Musil—one that is introspective, reasoned, and logical and that asks questions about the nature of identity. Notice, also, the simplicity and directness of Musil's prose. *The Man without Qualities* is considered one of the literary masterpieces of the twentieth century, a book that represents modernism at its best. The first volume of the book (which is around two thousand pages long, and whose later chapters exist in many versions) was published in 1930, and other chapters were published over a number of years.

We will also see the difference between postmodernist and modernist novels later, in selections from James Joyce's modernist masterpiece *Ulysses* and Georges Perec's postmodernist masterpiece *Life: A User's Manual*.

21 ▶ Feminism and Capitalist Libertarianism

If one examines capitalist libertarianism, one is faced with a choice: either reject subconstructive theory or conclude that consciousness is used to oppress the proletariat. It could be said that many dematerialisms concerning capitalist libertarianism may be found.

Lyotard suggests the use of subconstructive theory to attack sexism. Therefore, the premise of neotextual dialectic theory states that expression must come from the collective unconscious, given that feminism is invalid.

Sartre promotes the use of subconstructive theory to analyse and read class. It could be said that in *Finnegan's Wake,* Joyce reiterates capitalist libertarianism; in *Ulysses*, however, he affirms feminism. Foucault uses the term "Sartreist absurdity" to denote the common ground between society and class. Thus, Humphrey, holds that we have to choose between feminism and predeconstructivist narrative.[1]

— K. WILHELM ABIAN, "Deconstructing Debord: Feminism and Subconstructive Theory," Department of Semiotics, Massachusetts Institute of Technology, Boston, 2002.

1. Humphrey, R. ed. (1987) *Subconstructive Theory in the Works of Spelling.* And/Or Press.

The essay you have just read is completely meaningless and was randomly generated by the Postmodernism Generator, available on the Internet. This generator takes a number of the terms used by postmodernist writers and writers on postmodernism and makes it possible to generate essays that use postmodernist jargon but are nothing but gobbledygook, meaningless essays that look like postmodernist writings but don't make any sense. These works are parodies of postmodernist writing—which means that, whatever else you want to say about postmodernism, it does have a stylistic identity, which enables parodists to imitate and ridicule it.

Some people suggest that all postmodernist writing is nonsense and that the postmodernists are having fun at everyone else's expense. Postmodernism is a big put-on, they say, a game that certain writers play pretending to be serious. A communications scholar, Horace Newcomb, who teaches at the University of Texas, once wrote to me that there's no such thing as postmodernism:

> I consider it [postmodernism] mainly a matter of faith and do not personally believe in its existence. I think of it as the discovery by intellectuals of the practice of working class experience throughout the ages, and am somewhat resentful of the (generally) self-serving "theorizing" that accompanies discussions of this topic.

So there you are—a suggestion that postmodernism has an elitist bias to it and provides a way for intellectuals to snub their noses at middle- and working-class people who love Disneyland and shopping malls, reveling in forms of mass and popular culture that elitists, hiding under the cover of postmodernist thought, sneer at. In this view, postmodernism is the wolf of elitism in the sheep's clothing of cultural criticism.

The essay quoted in this selection, like many messages on the Internet, also has something of a fugitive nature. I downloaded it from the Internet but was unable to find it when I went searching for it later.

In general usage ... modernism describes that art (not just literature) which sought to break with what had become the dominant and dominating conventions of nineteenth-century art and culture. The most important of these conventions was REALISM: the modernist artist no longer saw the highest test of his or her art as that of verisimilitude. This does not mean that all modernist art gave up the attempt to understand or represent the extra-literary world, but that it rejected those nineteenth-century standards which had hardened into unquestioned conventions. Instead, the modernist art-work is possessed, typically, of a self-reflexive element: we may lose ourselves in the fictional "world," of, say, *Pride and Prejudice* when reading Jane Austen's novel, but when reading James Joyce's *Ulysses* or Virginia Woolf's *The Waves*, we are made conscious that we are reading a novel. . . . This does not mean that all modernist art gave up the attempt to understand or represent the extra-literary world, but that it rejected those nineteenth-century standards which had hardened into unquestioned conventions. . . . David Harvey has argued that modernism took on multiple perspectivism and RELATIVISM as its epistemology for revealing "what it still took to be the true nature of a unified, though complex, underlying reality. . . . Postmodernism, in contrast, tends to retain the relativism while abandoning the belief in the unified underlying reality. . . . For the modernist, therefore, human beings are doomed to exist in a state of social—and even existential—fragmentation, while yearning (unlike the postmodernist) to escape from this situation. Here the influence of Freud is probably important, for Freud turned the attention of many writers inward, towards subjective experience rather than the objective world. On the one hand, this led to the development or refinement of important new techniques: Joyce's and Wolf's development of internal monologue and stream-of-consciousness, Eliot's refinement of the dramatic monologue. But it also tied in with a pessimistic belief in the unbridgeability of the gap between subjective experience and an objective world, the belief that "It is impossible to say just what I mean!"

— JEREMY HAWTHORN, *A Concise Glossary of Contemporary Literary Theory,* 3d ed. (London: Arnold, 1998), 139–141.

The term "modernism" was coined in the third century and probably was used to refer to some break with ancient classical styles of literary and visual art. In its contemporary usage, it is often used to describe literary works that have some of the characteristics or stylistic elements that postmodernism rejected: a fascination with the self, an experimental approach to writing, a sense that reality exists and we can know it.

In 1924 Virginia Woolf, an important modernist writer, asserted that "in or about December, 1910, human character changed.... All human relations have shifted—those between masters and servants, husbands and wives, parents and children. And when human relations change there is at the same time a change in religion, conduct, politics and literature." She was alluding to the development of the modernist sensibility, which, she suggested, led to all kinds of other changes. The same kind of argument is made by postmodernists, who would suggest that in or around 1960, there was another monumental change or seismic shift—whatever you will—in our sensibilities from modernism to postmodernism and that this change is reflected in the works of writers, artists, architects and other creative people and has also had an impact on just about every aspect of our culture and society. It affects everything from the buildings we live in and see to our sense of identity, from our fashions to our entertainments.

Some theorists argue that what we call postmodernism is really just a version of modernism, just a form of the avant-garde, or just the reflection of the "cultural logic" of our late-capitalist economic system. A postmodernist might argue that postmodernism is anything you want it to be.

Freud

Critique of Fredric Jameson

In *The Cultural Logic of Late Capitalism,* Jameson posits that the modernist era, in contrast to that of the postmodern, both manifests an exemplary engagement of satiric interpretation and demonstrates an inherent need for universal norms within a parodic dynamic. According to Jameson, the modernist relies upon an implied expression of these norms in order to create an emergent sense of authenticity and originality such as the individual or personal style, "the Faulknerian long sentence." The personal style thus creates a satiric or critical space whereby it both reiterates and refigures aesthetic universal norms. The result is parody. As Jameson asserts, "all [of] these [parodic poses] strike one as somehow characteristic, insofar as they ostentatiously deviate from a norm which then reasserts itself . . . by a systematic mimicry of their willful eccentricities." . . . Modernist parody then, for Jameson, consists of a dialectic relation between what are held to be accepted, aesthetic universal norms and personal styles; the modernist artist simultaneously asserts both difference from and similarity to aesthetic currency in order to create parody.

In the postmodern, however, Jameson conversely finds that pastiche, in contrast to parody, proliferates due to an "unavailability of personal style." Drawing from Michel Foucault's critique of subjectivity and Jean Baudrillard's notion of the death of the subject through an enslavement to mass-media, Jameson argues that postmodern pastiche signifies that individualism, as defined during modernism, is dead. As he asserts, "Postmodern . . . signals . . . the end of the bourgeois ego [and] the end, for example, of style, in the sense of the unique and the personal, the end of the distinctive individual brushstroke." . . . Jameson thus argues that in a climate of media-enslaved, uncritical minds incapable of empowering subjectivity, pastiche thrives; postmodern uses of pastiche reflect the extent to which culture and the individual have become media-dominated. . . . Jameson further rationalizes that postmodern usage of pastiche also derives from a "sense in which the artists and writers of the present will no longer be able to invent new styles and worlds—they've already been invented; only a limited number of combinations are possible; the most unique ones have been thought of already." . . . Thus art becomes artifice, an endless recycling of the past, or "Modernist styles . . . become postmodernist codes." . . . In this way Jameson explains an expanded market for nostalgia and an obsessive reinterpretation of the past in postmodern fiction, film, video, art, and architecture. According to Jameson, consumer capitalism and the resultant commodification of culture have destroyed the ability of contemporary culture to produce original statements.

The commodification of culture and the increasing vacuum of a recycled past has also resulted in what Jameson terms a schizophrenic disposition within postmodern space. For Jameson, postmodern schizophrenia derives from a lack of historicity, or the disappearance of a sense of history due to postmodern recyclings of the past.

— MARCI SAFRAN, "Jameson, Jencks, and Juniors: Generation X as Critical Paradigm," *[Im]positions,* no. 1 (December 1996), www.gwu.edu/~position/marci.html [accessed November 21, 2002].

Here we find a discussion of the idea of one of the more celebrated analysts of postmodernism, Fredric Jameson. Pastiche, the use of elements taken from elsewhere, is intimately connected to postmodernism. In fact, one might argue that postmodernism and pastiche are, for all practical purposes, joined at the hip. The eclecticism that Lyotard wrote about earlier, the postmodern fascination with mass media (which is, from Jameson's perspective, a pastiche), and the alleged inability of postmodern artists to think up anything new or original all are connected to the pastiche, to the blendings of various elements into something else, but not necessarily something "new."

According to the Russian literary theorist and critic M. M. Bakhtin, all communication is essentially dialogical. This means that when we write or speak, according to Bakhtin, we always do so with a particular audience in mind, and our writing or speech is always tied to, and based to varying degrees upon, ideas and thoughts that have been communicated in the past. This means that the concept of dialogue is very important and, Bakhtin suggests, is a more useful and correct way of understanding communication than monologue, which gives primacy to the person doing the writing and thinking and creating.

What we write or say, for example, is intimately connected to our audience and the responses we can expect from them. (This dialogic process goes on whenever we write or talk, or, by extension, do any kind of creative activity.) We must keep in mind two important phenomena: First, the historical past has an impact on our ideas and on what we create; and, second, the future and the responses we can anticipate from our audience (real or imagined) affect what we do.

As Bakhtin writes in *The Dialogic Imagination* (1981: 279, 280), all our discourse is directed toward that which has already been uttered and toward an answer that we expect will be generated by our discourse. In our conversations, what we say always involves what has been said and an answer we anticipate.

Thus, the analogy we should make to understand communication and, in particular, the creation of texts, Bakhtin tells us, is that of dialogue and not monologue. Conversation, not monologism (or talking to oneself), is the basic metaphor.

Works of art—novels, films, poems, paintings, plays, and so on—are, then, suspended between the past and the future. That is, they are intertextual, in that they are affected to varying degrees by texts that have preceded them, texts that have to varying degrees affected their creators. Dialogism gives us new insights into the role of intertextuality in the creative process and into the role the audience plays in communication, whether it be conversation or the creation of artistic texts.

We also see how important the cultural context is for artists of all kinds. Whether they are conscious of it or not, artists are profoundly affected by their social and cultural milieux and by the texts and other creative works that already exist. These texts cast a shadow on, or provide a frame of reference (when not providing actual models) for, all works being created at a given moment.

24 The Postmodernization of Culture

Postmodern thought is characterized by a loss of belief in an objective world and an incredulity toward meta-narratives of legitimation. With a delegitimation of global systems of thought, there is no foundation to secure a universal and objective *reality.* There is today a growing public acknowledgment that "Reality isn't what it used to be." . . . In philosophy there is a departure from the belief in one true reality—subjectively copied in our heads by perception or objectively represented by scientific models. . . . There exists no pure uninterpreted datum; all facts embody theory.

Postmodernization of culture is best understood as an extension and intensification of differentiation, rationalization and commodification which dissolves the regional stability of modern culture and reverses its priorities. . . . Value-spheres become hyperdifferentiated, that is, their internal boundaries multiply to the point of fragmentation. As the particular genre, or style, becomes the unit of production and consumption, we orient ourselves to nostalgic classicism rather than "Art," to heavy metal rather than "Music" or to nineteenth-century women novelists rather than "Literature." The eventual effect of hyperdifferentiation is to set loose cultural "fragments" of intense symbolic power which transgresses the boundaries between value-spheres and between culture and other subsystems.

— STEPHEN CROOK, JAN PAKULSKI, and MALCOLM WATERS,
  Postmodernization: Change in Advanced Society (London: Sage,
  1992), 32, 36.

The authors of this selection discuss an important aspect of postmodernism—the way it involves a hyperdifferentiation, an overspecificity in cultural taste, so that one no longer listens to music but to heavy metal or reads literature but, instead, nineteenth-century women novelists. This shows how the fragmentation that is connected with postmodern culture plays out in the spheres of taste and consumption. There is also the matter of the way postmodernism forces us to interpret all data by tying it to some theory we hold. "There is no uninterpreted datum," our authors tell us. If "all facts embody theory," in essence, there are no facts per se, only facts that a theory we hold at a particular moment in time tells us are facts.

We can also regard this phenomenon as connected to consumption and suggest that we are pushing consumption to higher levels of importance and now are making more and more distinctions among products and services we purchase. This may be connected to our lack of coherent identity. We seek products to reinforce and affirm whatever identity we have chosen at a given moment. Since our identities are connected to the things we buy, the more identities we take on over time, the more things we need to purchase.

[8] Postmodern theory that is not seeking to simply appropriate the experience of "otherness" in order to enhance its discourse or to be radically chic should not separate the "politics of difference" from the politics of racism. To take racism seriously one must consider the plight of underclass people of color, a vast majority of whom are black. For African-Americans our collective condition prior to the advent of postmodernism and perhaps more tragically expressed under current postmodern conditions has been and is characterized by continued displacement, profound alienation and despair. Writing about blacks and postmodernism, Cornel West describes our collective plight: There is increasing class division and differentiation, creating on the one hand a significant black middle-class, highly anxiety-ridden, insecure, willing to be co-opted and incorporated into the powers that be, concerned with racism to the degree that it poses constraints on upward social mobility; and, on the other, a vast and growing black underclass, an underclass that embodies a kind of walking nihilism of pervasive drug addiction, pervasive alcoholism, pervasive homicide, and an exponential rise in suicide. Now because of the deindustrialization, we also have a devastated black industrial working class. We are talking here about tremendous hopelessness. This hopelessness creates longing for insight and strategies for change that can renew spirits and reconstruct grounds for collective black liberation struggle. The overall impact of the postmodern condition is that many other groups now share with black folks a sense of deep alienation, despair, uncertainty, loss of a sense of grounding, even if it is not informed by shared circumstance. Radical postmodernism calls attention to those sensibilities which are shared across the boundaries of class, gender, and race, and which could be fertile ground for the construction of empathy—ties that would promote recognition of common commitments and serve as a base for solidarity and coalition.

[9] "Yearning" is the word that best describes a common psychological state shared by many of us, cutting across boundaries of race, class, gender, and sexual practice. Specifically in relation to the postmodernist deconstruction of "master" narratives, the yearning that wells in the hearts and minds of those whom such narratives have silenced is the longing for critical voice. It is no accident that "rap" has usurped the primary position of R&B music among young black folks as the most desired sound, or that it began as a form of "testimony" for the underclass. It has enabled underclass black youth to develop a critical voice, as a group of young black men told me, a "common literacy." Rap projects a critical voice, explaining, demanding,

urging. Working with this insight in his essay "Putting the Pop Back into Postmodernism," Lawrence Grossberg comments: The postmodern sensibility appropriates practices as boasts that announce their own—and consequently our own—existence, like a rap song boasting of the imaginary (or real—it makes no difference) accomplishments of the rapper.

— bell hooks, "Postmodern Blackness," *Postmodern Culture* 1, no. 1 (September 1990), www.sas.upenn.edu/African_Studies/ Articles_Gen/Postmodern_Blackness_18270.html.

bell hooks—that's the way she spells her name—considers the relationship between postmodernism and racism directed toward people of color, and, in particular, black men and women. She sees the development of rap music in political terms. It represents the means by which black people can make their voices heard—asserting their own individuality and calling attention, as "critical voices," to social and political problems. She contends that there is in contemporary America (and other countries as well, by implication) a large black underclass of people who have been left out of the rise to middle-class status. Rap, then, has an important political significance, though many of its fans may not be aware of this, and is more than mere entertainment.

26 ◢ Punk and Postmodernism

Latter-day punks such as the Riot Grrrls still battle with that authoritarianism, now a virtual fascism bashing any choices besides domesticity for women (whether Hillary Rodham Clinton or pregnant teenagers), any resistance against big business (whether environmentalism or organized labor), every nonwhite person guilty of poverty (whether black or Latino), and any trace of deviance (whether in ideology or sexual orientation). The various cultural conflicts of the 1990s might be summed up under one "general heading: the culture of self-satisfaction versus the culture of the dissatisfied."

From the postmodern view, however, punk was the last hurrah for any faith that popular music could have a genuinely radical impact on even a small portion of its audience. In essence, presumably, postmodernism fully arrived in rock and roll when punk lost its momentum around 1981, with the advent of New Pop posers (e.g., "haircut bands" such as Duran Duran) and a new cable channel reliant on their videos, MTV. If punk achieved mass popularity a decade later, it did so under very different circumstances, when "alternative" music was well incorporated into the music industry. The second coming of punk could only amount to a trivial shift in poses for those with more outrageous tastes. Someone like me (or Greil Marcus or Jon Savage) who continues to dwell on the possibilities I felt in 1977, therefore, is guilty of bringing "pop history [to] a halt" and ducking the demise of "authenticity" in music in the 1980s, claims Steve Redhead. (As Dominic Strinati points out, though, musical authenticity has never really existed, except in mythologies about past innocence and in marketing strategies exploiting that nostalgia.) The terms *rebellion* and *resistance* have supposedly become irrelevant since punk's heyday, making postpunk synonymous with postmodern (the view of a number of the academics . . .).

But the long life of punk, I argue, simply reflects the fact that punk has been the persistent nemesis of the authoritarianism that emerged in the 1970s and expanded and intensified throughout the 1980s and 1990s. (That the authoritarians still bash around the 1960s, while the 1970s are popularly associated with *The Brady Bunch,* indicates how long they've held the upper hand.) The large amount of angry music at present reflects the steadily worsening situation since the original moment of punk, which followed shortly on the beginning of Western capitalism's all-out assault on its domestic adversaries in 1973, with the shock of the Arab oil embargo and the realization that the postwar economic expansion would not go on forever. David Harvey's *The Condition of Postmodernity* (1989) provides a good summary account of the transition in 1973 to the insecure world of "flexible accumu-lation," in which the financial system has become increasingly detached from real production (and his point is to give a more concrete explanation of recent cultural and social changes than talismanic invocation of postmod-ernism). With the deliberate contraction of economic opportunity on the part of the plutocratic class—resulting in such lunatic viciousness as the Federal Reserve Board keeping at least eight million people unemployed at all times while politicians seek to starve them for not working—there has under-standably been an expansion of anger in the music of the increasingly large number of economically obsolete young people.

— NEIL NEHRING, *Popular Music, Gender, and Postmodernism: Anger Is an Energy* (Thousand Oaks, Calif.: Sage, 1997), xxvi–xxvii.

Nehring, like bell hooks, suggests that punk music—a precursor to rap—had a radical agenda and represented an attack on the authoritarianism that he felt was becoming an ever more important aspect of life in America in the sev-enties. His words about the postwar expansion not being able to go on forever have a particular resonance to America in 2002, when the dot-com bubble burst and the American economy tanked. In a sense, America in 2002 is very similar to America in the seventies, when the economy suddenly fell apart and a huge number of people found themselves without jobs and possibilities.

What is worse, Nehring suggests, is that we now have many "economically obsolete young people" who are very angry. Thus, punk for a number of years was an outlet for this anger, but it did not have a radicalizing impact on any appreciable number of young people. Whether rap will have the desired effect is dif-ficult to say at this time. Nehring is not very optimistic that his radical agenda has much chance of being implemented. One can only wonder what he would have said had he writ-ten his book after September 11, 2001, when the authori-tarianism of the government—or, to be more specific, the power of the attorney general and various law enforcement agencies, under the cover of security—seems to have grown considerably.

27   "Sorties" by Hélène Cixous

Where is she?
Activity/passivity,
Sun/Moon
Culture/Nature
Day/Night

Father/Mother
Head/Heart
Intelligible/Sensitive
Logos/Pathos

Form, convex, step, advance, seed, progress.
Matter, concave, ground—which supports the step, receptacle.

<u> Man </u>
Woman

Always the same metaphor: we follow it, it transports us, in all of its forms, wherever a discourse is organized. The same thread, or double tress leads us, whether we are reading or speaking, through literature, philosophy, criticism, centuries of representation, of reflection.
    Thought has always worked by opposition,
    Speech/Writing
    High/Low

By dual, *hierarchized* oppositions. Superior/Inferior. Myths, legends, books. Philosophical systems. Wherever an ordering intervenes, a law organizes the thinkable by (dual, irreconcilable; or mitigable, dialectical) oppositions. And all the couples of oppositions are *couples*. Does this mean something? Is the fact that logocentrism subjects thought—all of the concepts, the codes, the values—to a two-term system, related to "the" couple man/woman?
    Nature/History
    Nature/Art,
    Nature/Mind,
    Passion/Action.

Theory of culture, theory of society, the ensemble of symbolic systems—art, religion, family, language,—everything elaborates the same systems. And the movement by which each opposition is set up to produce meaning is the movement by which the couple is destroyed. A universal battlefield. Each time a war breaks out. Death is always at work.
    Father/son   Relationships of authority, of privilege, of force.
    Logos/writing   Relationships: opposition, conflict, relief,
    Master/slave   Violence. Repression.

And we perceive that the "victory" always amounts to the same thing: it is hierarchized. The hierarchization subjects the entire conceptual organization to man. A male privilege, which can be seen in the opposition by which it sustains itself between *activity* and *passivity.* Traditionally, the question of sexual difference is coupled with the same opposition: activity/passivity.

That goes a long way. If we examine the history of philosophy—in so far as philosophical discourse orders and reproduces all thought—we perceive that: it is marked by an absolute constant, the orchestrator of values, which is precisely the opposition activity/passivity.

In philosophy, woman is always on the side of passivity. Every time the question comes up; when we examine kinship structures; whenever a family model is brought into play; in fact as the ontological question is raised; as soon as you ask yourself what is meant by the question "What is it?"; as soon as there is a will to say something. A will: desire, authority—you examine that, and you are led right back—to the father. You can even fail to notice that there's no place at all for women in the operation! In the extreme, the world of "being" can function to the exclusion of the mother—provided there is something of the maternal: and it is the father then who acts—is—the mother. Either the woman is passive; or she doesn't exist. What is left is unthinkable, unthought of. She does not enter into the oppositions, she is not coupled with the father (who is coupled with the son).

— HÉLÈNE CIXOUS, "Sorties," in *Modern Criticism and Theory: A Reader,* ed. David Lodge (London: Longman, 1988), 286–87.

This selection by Hélène Cixous, a professor at the University of Paris in Vincennes and an internationally known feminist, calls to mind the selection from Ferdinand de Saussure, in which he argues that concepts have no meaning in themselves but only take on meaning differentially. Cixous starts "Sorties" with a list of polar oppositions such as activity/passivity, which finally leads to an opposition relating men and women—one that she presents in a different manner from her earlier ones.

This opposition puts man over woman and is meant to signify, typographically as well as socially, the relationship between men and women:

Man
Woman

If you look at the list of polar oppositions with which Cixous starts this essay, you can see that the masculine entities—activity, sun, culture, day, father—are on the left, and the feminine entities—passivity, moon, nature, night, mother—are on the right. She points out that traditionally men are defined as active and women are defined as passive and that society, where men dominate, is seen in hierarchical terms, with males on the top and women on the bottom. "Either woman is passive; or she doesn't exist." Cixous argues, elsewhere in this article, that a new order is needed—one involving a radical and structural transformation of society. When this happens, she asserts, "The general logic of difference would no longer fit into the opposition that still dominates." For the moment, however, she suggests, her somewhat utopian hopes are far from being realized. We continue to flounder about, she laments, "in the Old order."

Images and Simulations

Thus perhaps at stake has always been the murderous capacity of images, murderers of the real, murderers of their own model, as the Byzantine icons could murder the divine identity. To this murderous capacity is opposed the dialectical capacity of representations as a visible and intelligible mediation of the Real. All of Western faith and good faith was engaged in this wager on representation: That a sign could refer to the depth of meaning, that a sign could exchange for meaning, and that something could guarantee this exchange—God, of course. But what if God himself can be simulated, that is to say, reduced to the signs which attest his existence? Then the whole system becomes weightless, it is no longer anything but a gigantic simulacrum—not unreal, but a simulacrum, never again exchanging for what is real, but exchanging in itself, in an uninterrupted circuit without reference or circumference.

So it is with simulation, insofar as it is opposed to representation. The latter starts from the principle that the sign and the real are equivalent (even if this equivalence is utopian, it is a fundamental axiom). Conversely, simulation starts from the utopia of this principle of equivalence, from the radical negation of the sign as value, from the sign as reversion and death sentence of every reference. Whereas representation tries to absorb simulation by interpreting it as false representation, simulation envelops the edifice of representation as itself a simulacrum. This would be the successive phases of the image:

1. it is the reflection of a basic reality.
2. it masks and perverts a basic reality.
3. it masks the absence of a basic reality.
4. it bears no relation to any reality whatever: it is its own pure simulacrum.

— JEAN BAUDRILLARD, "The Evil Demon of Images and the Precession of Simulacra," in *Postmodernism: A Reader,* ed. Thomas Docherty (New York: Columbia University Press, 1993), 194.

This selection by Baudrillard deals with his analysis of the power of images in generating simulations and a hyperreality in postmodern societies—one of the dominant themes in his writing on the subject. Just as fish do not realize they are in water, we do not realize that we are living in a gigantic hyperreality, a world of images that reflect other images endlessly and that, ultimately, in a process he describes, bear no relation to reality.

Baudrillard distinguishes between representation and simulation. Representation sees the sign as tied to something real. (Saussure, one of the fathers of semiotics, said a sign is composed of a signifier and a signified, a sound-image and a concept or an object. Signs are always connected to things.) Simulation moves from being a reflection of reality to being something that has no connection with reality, and that is the world, he tells us, that we now live in—in our postmodern societies, in our world of simulations.

In his book *America*, Baudrillard argues that:

> America is neither dream nor reality. It is a hyperreality. . . . Everything here is real and pragmatic, and yet is the stuff of dreams too. It may be that the truth of America can only be seen by a European, since he alone will discover here the perfect simulacrum—that of the immanence and material transcription of all values. The Americans, for their part, have no sense of simulation. They are themselves simulation in its most developed state, but they have no language in which to describe it, since they themselves are the model. (1988: 28, 29)

If Baudrillard is correct, America is the most advanced postmodernist society in the world, but because we are so immersed in it, we don't realize what we have created and what effects this postmodern society we have created has upon us.

29 Postmodernist Architecture

I would define postmodernism ... as double coding—the combination of modern techniques with something else (usually traditional building) in order for architecture to communicate with the public and a concerned minority—usually other architects. The point of this double coding was itself double. Modern architecture had failed to remain credible partly because it didn't communicate with its ultimate users—the main argument of my book *The Language of Post-Modern Architecture*—and partly because it didn't make effective links with the city and history. Thus the solution I perceived and defined as postmodern: an architecture that was professionally based and popular as well as one that was based on new techniques and old patterns. Double coding, to simplify, means both elite/popular culture and new/old and there are compelling reasons for these opposite pairings. Today's postmodern architects were trained by modernists, and are committed to using contemporary technology as well as facing current social reality. These commitments are enough to distinguish them from revivalists or traditionalists, a point worth stressing since it creates their hybrid language, the style of postmodern architecture. The same is not completely true of postmodern artists and writers who may use traditional techniques of narrative and representation in a more straightforward way. Yet all the creators who could be called postmodern keep something of a modern sensibility—some intention which distinguishes their work from that of revivalists—whether this is irony, parody, displacement, complexity, eclecticism, realism, or any number of contemporary tactics and goals. Postmodernism has the essential double meaning: the continuation of modernism and its transcendence. . . .

Modernism failed as mass-housing and city building partly because it failed to communicate with its inhabitants and users who might not have liked the style, understood what it meant, or even known how to use it. Hence the double coding, the essential definition of postmodernism, has been used as a strategy for communicating on various levels at once.

Virtually every postmodern architect—Robert Venturi, Hans Hollein, Charles Moore, Robert Stern, Michael Graves, Arata Isozaki are the notable examples—use popular and elitist signs in their work to achieve quite different ends, and their styles are essentially hybrid. . . . In any complex building, in any large city building such as an office, there will be varying tastes and functions that have to be articulated and these will inevitably lead, if the architect follows these hints, toward an eclectic style.

— CHARLES JENCKS, "Postmodern vs. Late Modern," in *Zeitgeist in Babel: The Post-Modernist Controversy*, ed. Ingeborg Hoesterey (Bloomington: Indiana University Press, 1991), 4–8.

Jencks, an architect who has written extensively on postmodernism, offers us a slightly different way of understanding what it is. Postmodernism involves what he calls "double coding," which we can take to mean the use of different aesthetic modes in the same work. Thus a building can have certain features generally connected with modernism but also other features tied to a different style, emerging, with its combination of styles, as a postmodernist building. This combination of elite/popular and new/old leads to architecture that is mindful of the many different groups and subcultures that will use the building. Postmodern architecture becomes, then, a reflection of societies that now are multicultured and multiethnic with various levels of taste, culture, and sophistication.

Postmodernism, from this point of view, has its roots in American democratic egalitarianism and is not a joke that artists, writers, and architects are playing on everyone else, as elitists might suggest. The stylistic eclecticism found in postmodern architecture, then, is a reflection of a democratic society that wants buildings to work for many different kinds of people and does not reflect a loss of identity and a lack of center in people. In his article Jencks contrasts postmodern architecture with the failure of some modernist architecture—the giant slabs of apartments that were built when modernist architectural styles were dominant. People sometimes found these buildings alienating and intolerable, and eventually some were blown up, to be replaced by housing, sometimes with postmodernist stylistic elements, that had a more human scale to it.

30 ▸ Notes on Camp

Though I am speaking about sensibility only—and about a sensibility that, among other things, converts the serious into the frivolous—these are grave matters. Most people think of sensibility or taste as the realm of purely subjective preferences, those mysterious attractions, mainly sensual, that have not been brought under the sovereignty of reason. They *allow* that considerations of taste play a part in their reactions to people and to works of art. But this attitude is naive. And even worse. To patronize the faculty of taste is to patronize oneself. For taste governs every free—as opposed to rote—human response. Nothing is more decisive. There is taste in people, visual taste, taste in emotion—and there is taste in acts, taste in morality. Intelligence, as well, is really a kind of taste: taste in ideas. (One of the facts to be reckoned with is that taste tends to develop very unevenly. It's rare that the same person has good visual taste *and* good taste in people *and* taste in ideas.)

Taste has no system and no proofs. But there is something like a logic of taste: the consistent sensibility which underlies and gives rise to a certain taste. A sensibility is almost, but not quite, ineffable. Any sensibility which can be crammed into the mold of a system, or handled with the rough tools of proof, is no longer a sensibility at all. It has hardened into an idea....

To snare a sensibility in words, especially one that is alive and powerful, one must be tentative and nimble. The form of jottings, rather than an essay (with its claim to a linear, consecutive argument), seemed more appropriate for getting down something of this particular fugitive sensibility. It's embarrassing to be solemn and treatise-like about Camp. One runs the risk of having, oneself, produced a very inferior piece of Camp....

1. To start very generally: Camp is a certain mode of aestheticism. It is *one* way of seeing the world as an aesthetic phenomenon. That way, the way of Camp, is not in terms of beauty, but in terms of the degree of artifice, of stylization.

2. To emphasize style is to slight content, or to introduce an attitude which is neutral with respect to content. It goes without saying that the Camp sensibility is disengaged, depoliticized—or at least apolitical.

3. Not only is there a Camp vision, a Camp way of looking at things. Camp is as well a quality discoverable in objects and the behavior of persons. There are "campy" movies, clothes, furniture. popular songs, novels, people, buildings. This distinction is important. True, the Camp eye has the power to transform experience. But not everything can be seen as Camp. Its not *all* in the eye of the beholder.

— SUSAN SONTAG, *Against Interpretation* (New York: Laurel Books, 1969), 278–79.

Sontag's essay "Notes on Camp" may be seen as a precursor to the kind of writing found on postmodernism. Her essay deals with a certain sensibility—which she calls "Camp" and which may be seen as, in essence, postmodern. Wherever one finds the word "Camp" in this essay, one could substitute the word "postmodern" and the essay would still make sense. Camp, Sontag argues, reflects a certain sensibility—one that is best captured by random jottings (similar, perhaps, to a pastiche?) rather than reasoned argument, since logical argument about camp would be, itself, camp. Sontag's essay, written in 1964, is one of the earlier statements that reflects the impact of the postmodern sensibility both in its style and in its subject.

Later in the essay Sontag argues against assuming that camp is necessarily bad, though there is lots of bad camp that she describes as kitsch. She offers fifty-eight notes on camp, the last of which has a definite postmodern ironical ring: "The ultimate Camp statement: it's good because it's awful. . . . Of course, one can't always say that. Only under certain conditions, which I've tried to sketch in these notes."

It is possible, on the basis of her essay, to suggest that Sontag is a proto-postmodernist, or, even better, a pre-postmodernist, if that makes sense.

James Joyce's *Ulysses*

nothing like nature the wild mountains then the sea and the waves rushing then the beautiful country with fields of oats and wheat and all kinds of things and all the fine cattle going about that would do your heart good to see rivers and lakes and flowers all sorts of shapes and smells and colours springing up even out of the ditches primroses and violets nature it is as for them saying theres no God I wouldnt give a snap of my two fingers for all their learning why dont they go and create something I often asked him atheists or whatever they call themselves go and wash the cobbles off themselves first then they go howling for the priest and they dying and why because theyre afraid of hell on account of their bad conscience ah yes I know them well who was the first person in the universe before there was anybody that made it all who ah that they dont know neither do I so there you are they might as well try to stop the sun from rising tomorrow the sun shines for you he said the day we were lying among the rhododendrons on Howth head in the grey tweed suit and his straw hat the day I got him to propose to me yes first I gave him the bit of seedcake out of my mouth and it was leapyear like now yes 16 years ago my God after that long kiss I near lost my breath yes he said I was a flower of the mountain yes so we are flowers all a womans body yes that was one true thing he said in his life and the sun shines for you today yes that was why I liked him because I saw he understood or felt what a woman is and I knew I could always get round him and I gave him all the pleasure I could leading him on till he asked me to say yes and I wouldnt answer first only looked out over the sea and the sky I was thinking of so many things he didnt know of Mulvey and Mr Stanhope and Hester and father and old captain Groves and the sailors playing all birds fly and I say stoop and washing up dishes they called it on the pier and the sentry in front of the governors house with the thing round his white helmet poor devil half roasted and the Spanish girls laughing in their shawls and their tall combs and the auctions in the morning the Greeks and the jews and the Arabs and the devil knows who else from all the ends of Europe and Duke street and the fowl market all clucking outside Larby Sharons and the poor donkeys slipping half asleep and the vague fellows in the cloaks asleep . . .

— JAMES JOYCE, *Ulysses* (New York: Random House, 1942), 767

This selection, the next-to-the last page in Joyce's monumental novel *Ulysses*, gives a good idea of the experimental style he used. Joyce is one of the most important modernist novelists, and his novel is considered by literary critics to be one of the greatest novels of the twentieth century. It deals with one day in the life of Leopold Bloom, whose wife Molly has a fifty-four-page stream-of-consciousness fantasy, devoid of any punctuation, that concludes the novel. The selection above is from this passage. Censors in America tried to prevent the book from being published here, arguing that it was pornographic and obscene, but in a finding on December 6, 1933, Judge John M. Woolsey lifted the ban on *Ulysses* and Random House proceeded to publish it. Woolsey asked some literary experts for their opinions and then concluded, in his finding, that *Ulysses* "did not tend to excite sexual impulses or lustful thoughts but that its net effect on them was only that of a somewhat tragic and very powerful commentary on the inner lives of men and women."

It is useful to keep this passage in mind when reading the next selection, which is from Georges Perec's postmodern novel, *Life: A User's Manual*. Both *Ulysses* and *Life: A User's Manual* are remarkable works, which, I believe you will be able to see, reflect different mentalities at work. Both of these novels are large, complex, "experimental" works, and each of them is a good representative of the mind-set and stylistic elements associated with either modernism or postmodernism. *Ulysses* deals with one day in the life of Leopold Bloom, but that one day and Bloom's experiences offer insights into the human condition.

The man facing the others is Japanese. His name is Ashikage Yoshimitsu. He belongs to a sect founded in 1960 in Manila by a deep-sea fisherman, a post-office employee, and a butcher's mate. The Japanese name of the sect is "Shira Nami," which means "The White Wave;" in French it is called "Les Trois Hommes Libres", or "The Three Free Men."

In the three years following the founding of the sect, each of these "three free men" managed to convert three others. The nine men of the second generation initiated twenty-seven over the next three years. The sixth level, in 1975, numbered seven hundred and twenty-nine members, including Ashikage Yoshimitsu, who was given the task, along with some other members, of spreading the new faith in the West. Initiation into the sect of The Three Free Men is long, hard, and very expensive, but it does not seem that Yoshimitsu had much difficulty in finding three converts rich enough to set aside the time and the money obligatorily required for such an enterprise.

The novices are at the very first stage of initiation and have to overcome preliminary trials in which they must absorb themselves in the contemplation of a perfectly trivial mental or material object to such a degree as to become oblivious to all feeling, even to extreme pain. . . .

As for the object of meditation, each has a different one. The first novice, who has the exclusive sales rights in France for the products of a Swedish manufacturer of hanging tiles, has to solve a puzzle presented to him in the form of a small white card on which the following question has been finely handwritten in violet ink:

Who loves to eat her fill along Aymen?

above which a bow has been drawn around the figure 6.

The second pupil is German, the owner of a baby-wear factory in Stuttgart. He has in front of him, placed on a steel cube, a piece of flotsam of a shape quite closely resembling a ginseng root. The third—who is French, and a star singer—faces a voluminous treatise on the culinary arts, the sort of book that usually goes on sale for the Christmas season. The book is placed on a music stand. It is open at an illustration of a reception given in 1890 by Lord Radnor in the drawing rooms of Longford Castle. Printed on the left-hand page in a frame of *art nouveau* colophons and garland decorations is a recipe for:

STRAWBERRY CREAM

Take 10 oz, wild or cultivated strawberries.
Strain through a fine sieve. Mix in 3 oz. icing sugar.
Whip 1 pt cream until very firm and blend in the mixture.
Spoon the mixture from the bowl into small round paper cups,
and cool for two hours in a cellar that is not too cold.
To serve, place a large strawberry in each cup.

— GEORGES PEREC, *Life: A User's Manual,* trans. David Bellis
(Boston: Godine, 1978), 11–12.

Georges Perec's *Life: A User's Manual* is a large work that is generally recognized as one of the great postmodern novels. In this novel, Perec deals with the lives of the inhabitants of a building at 11 rue Simon-Crubellier in Paris, many of whom are very strange and unusual individuals. For example, one of the inhabitants, Bartlebooth, spends many years traveling around the world painting watercolor landscapes. He sends them back to France where they are attached to wood and made into puzzles. He returns to France, solves the puzzles, and then has the watercolors destroyed, so his whole life's work ends in nothing. There is a kind of game-playing mentality informing the novel—we find in it a kind of logic to the behavior of the characters, but everything is also rather crazy.

In the passage that comes after this selection, Perec calculates that by 2017 the Shira Nami cult will have a billion people, and by 2020 everyone in the world will belong to it. We find the use of logic and rationality in the service of absurd matters. In the best postmodern tradition, Perec also provides us with a recipe. In one of his novels, *The Void*, he has no e's in the entire work. The only e's in the novel are found on the title page, in his name. It is a remarkable feat, and a fine novel—but it is something, one might venture to suggest, that only a writer with a comic postmodernist sensibility, in love with games, would be interested in trying.

33

Disney and Postmodernism

Disney, the precursor, the grand initiator of the imaginary as virtual reality, is now in the process of capturing all the real world to integrate it into its synthetic universe, in the form of a vast "reality show" where reality itself becomes a spectacle [*vient se donner en spectacle*], where the real becomes a theme park. The transfusion of the real is like a blood transfusion, except that here it is a transfusion of real blood into the exsanguine universe of virtuality. After the prostitution of the imaginary, here is now the hallucination of the real in its ideal and simplified version.

At Disney World in Orlando, they are even building an identical replica of the Los Angeles Disneyland, as a sort of historical attraction to the second degree, a simulacrum to the second power. It is the same thing that CNN did with the Gulf War: a prototypical event which did not take place, because it took place in real time, in CNN's instantaneous mode. Today, Disney could easily revisit the Gulf War as a worldwide show. The Red Army choirs have already celebrated Christmas at Euro Disney. Everything is possible, and everything is recyclable in the polymorphous universe of virtuality. Everything can be bought over. There is no reason why Disney would not take over the human genome, which, by the way, is already being resequenced, to turn it into a genetic show. In the end [*au fond*], they would cryogenize the entire planet, just like Walt Disney himself who decided to be cryogenized in a nitrogen solution, waiting for some kind of resurrection in the real world. But there is no real world anymore, not even for Walt Disney. If one day he wakes up, he'll no doubt have the biggest surprise of his life. Meanwhile, from the bottom of his nitrogen solution he continues to colonize the world—both the imaginary and the real—in the spectral universe of virtual reality, inside which we all have become extras [*figurants*]. The difference is that when we put on our digital suits, plug in our sensorial captors, or press the keys of our virtual reality arcade, we enter live spectrality whereas Disney, the genial anticipator, has entered the virtual reality of death.

The New World Order is in a Disney mode. But Disney is not alone in this mode of cannibalistic attraction. We saw Benetton with his commercial campaigns, trying to recuperate the human drama of the news (AIDS, Bosnia, poverty, apartheid) by transfusing reality into a New Mediatic Figuration (a place where suffering and commiseration end in a mode of interactive resonance). The virtual takes over the real as it appears, and then replicates it without any modification [*le recrache tel quel*], in a *pret-a-porter* (ready-to-wear) fashion.

— JEAN BAUDRILLARD, "Disney World Company," *Libération* (Paris), March 4, 1996. Translated by François Debrix.

Baudrillard is very much interested in Disney and asserts that Disney, with his various enterprises, is an important cultural figure and has had an enormous impact on American culture and other cultures as well. As a matter of fact, Disney is colonizing and Disneyizing the entire world, Baudrillard contends. One question that the Disneyfication of the world suggests involves what is real and what is virtual or a simulation. Baudrillard is fascinated by Disney's quest for immortality—he has been cryogenized, or suspended in liquid nitrogen, in the hope that in the future he can be brought back to life. What all this suggests is that nothing is real, nothing has meaning anymore—even death can be countered, if you can afford to be cryogenized. The real has been supplanted by the virtual, and now, in our postmodern world, it is difficult to separate one from the other.

This is not a pipe

34

Postmodernism as Chaotic Critique

The problem is not that the postmodernist spirit lacks a critical impulse, but that critique is running rampant without political direction. Zygmunt Bauman, in *Intimations of Postmodernity,* describes how the new mood can appear to be one of "all-eroding, all dissolving *destructiveness*" (1992: viii; emphasis in original). He goes on: "The postmodern mind seems to condemn everything, propose nothing," as if "demolition is the only the job the postmodern mind seems to be good at" (p. ix). The genie of critique has escaped its bottle, and now, unstoppably, it darts hither and thither in random flights of mischief. It does not merely attack the ruling ideas, or the mass-produced ideas of economically organized popular culture. What Paul Ricoeur (1986) calls the "hermeneutics of suspicion" has become the prevailing mood. Every assertion of truth is to be the target of critique, for every such assertion, so it is alleged, makes claims which cannot be substantiated. Moreover, it is an exercise of power, for each claim about "the true," or "the real," asserts its own voice, and thereby suppresses alternative voices.

— HERBERT W. SIMONS and MICHAEL BILLIG, introduction to *After Postmodernism: Reconstructing Ideology Critique,* ed. Herbert W. Simons and Michael Billig (London: Sage, 1994), 6.

Is postmodernism essentially negative, finding lots of things to attack and very little to propose? That, in essence, is the argument made in this selection. Postmodernism has generally taken pride in its critical spirit, but according to the authors, the genie of postmodernist criticism has escaped from its bottle and now is suspicious of everything. We must keep in mind that postmodernism is, by definition, a refutation of modernist thought and culture, so there is something intrinsically negative or rejectionist in postmodernism.

The question that arises is, what does postmodernism have to offer as far as creating social and political institutions and keeping a society vibrant? On the personal level, one can get by with an ironic stance and a fascination with style, but a group of ironic, game-playing postmodernists isn't the same thing as a community. Of course, the postmodernist would argue that community is of little concern to them, just as being able to offer positive suggestions instead of critical opinions is of little interest.

35 ▸ A Postmodernist Hotel and Its Problems

Given the absolute symmetry of the four towers, it is quite impossible to get your bearings in this lobby; recently, color coding and directional signals have been added in a pitiful and revealing, rather desperate, attempt to restore the coordination of an older space. I will take as the most dramatic practical result of this spatial mutation the notorious dilemma of the shopkeepers on the various balconies: it has been obvious since the opening of the hotel in 1977 that nobody could ever find any of these stores, and unlikely to be as fortunate a second time; as a consequence, the commercial tenants are in despair and all the merchandise is marked down to bargain prices. When you recall that Portman is a businessman as well as an architect and millionaire developer, an artist who is at one and the same time a capitalist in his own right, one cannot but feel that here too something of a "return of the repressed" is involved.

So I come to my principal point here, that this latest mutation in space— postmodern hyperspace—has finally succeeded in transcending the capacities of the individual human body to locate itself, to organize its immediate surroundings perceptually, and cognitively to map its position in a mappable external world. It may now be suggested that this alarming disjunction point between the body and its built environment—which is to the initial bewilderment of the older modernism as the velocities of spacecraft to those of the automobile—can itself stand as the symbol and analogon of that ever sharper dilemma which is the incapacity of our minds, at least at present, to map the great global multinational and decentered communicational network in which we find ourselves caught as individual subjects.

— FREDRIC JAMESON, *Postmodernism or, The Cultural Logic of Late Capitalism* (Durham, N.C.: Duke University Press, 1991), 43–44.

This discussion of architect John Portman's postmodern Westin Bonaventure Hotel in Los Angeles offers a different perspective on postmodern architecture from the one Jencks takes in his article, which celebrates the democratic impulses in postmodern architecture. Postmodern hyperspace, Jameson argues, connects to a larger theme, the way individuals are unable to deal with "the great global multinational and decentered communicational network in which we find ourselves caught as individual subjects" (44).

The Bonaventure functions, Jameson asserts, as a signifier both of a mutation in architectural design and, analogously, of the new global communication networks found in postmodern societies. In both cases, individuals lose their ability to determine where they are and how to get to where they want to go.

His discussion of the Bonaventure Hotel occurs in a chapter on culture. Jameson argues that we have changed the way we relate to architectural spaces much more quickly than we have changed our psyches and our social systems. Jameson suggests that while postmodernism is "a cultural dominant," something that shapes attitudes, beliefs, values, and cultures, it is, in reality, only a manifestation of the latest form of multinational capitalism. Postmodernism, Jameson says, was preceded by realism, which was a reflection of market capitalism, and by modernism, which was a reflection of monopoly capitalism.

It is the Bonaventure Hotel in Los Angeles that Jameson selects as his example of a mutation in the way people in postmodern societies create architectural spaces. Jameson tells us that what we find in the Bonaventure is a total space that accurately reflects the consciousness of people living in postmodern societies. The Bonaventure represents a new way in which people congregate and move about, forming what Jameson describes as a "hypercrowd," one that is unable to negotiate the lobby of the Bonaventure in the same way that individuals find themselves unable to negotiate late capitalist postmodern societies in general. I should point out that some architects and critics have attacked Jameson's description of the Bonaventure as incorrect and inaccurate.

36

Postmodernism's Impact on Signs and Signifiers

Postmodernists such as Baudrillard celebrate the liberation of signs from dependency on well-defined signifieds. In part, this is viewed as a liberation from the strict confines of normative, foundationalist doctrines which themselves have historically led to tyranny and repression so many times. In part, too, this liberation celebrates the demise of bourgeois ideology which disappears in the "black hole" of omnivorous and voracious capitalist consumerism. The outcome of postmodernist cultural production has meant for many a liberation from the canons of tradition and the creation of a certain space within which free expression and free association can reign.

I [have] argued that culture in late capitalism doesn't quite fit the reductionist vision of postmodernists. Mass culture involves a three-way relation between use, exchange, and sign values. The extraction of the latter by mass culture industries who produce commodities for profit most often involves the stripping away of deep-level signifieds, or contextualized use values, and the marketing of the gutted shell of meaningful signs as images. The latter constitutes the elements of culture that bother postmodernists most, but free-floating signifiers represent only one aspect of culture. There is also an authentic sector that involves everyday practices which can manifest resistance. One important feature of the dynamic relation between subcultures and the dominant culture industry is the way the latter requires the everyday culture production, or the signifying practices of the former for its own commodity production. Reversing that process and reclaiming the stripped-away signifieds becomes, then, a type of cultural criticism, just as it may also protect us from the imperialistic demands of the dominant culture industries.

Postmodern critics, however, are not completely wrong. While all forms of authentic culture are not automatically coopted by the hyperreal image-inducing and -mediating process of the culture industry, there is ample evidence to suggest that image-driven culture affects individual self-expression and the grounds of meaning in daily life. Mass cultural production diverts our ability to place deep-level understandings on the images that are constantly valorized for us by that industry. In particular, there remains an often implicit acknowledgement that postmodernism, more so than previous cultural modes, subverts the desire for authenticity in everyday life. It is, in fact, the enemy of authenticity, poised as it is to pounce on any cultural form and strip its deep meanings bare for the benefit of handling a decontextualized and easily manipulatable signifier as some new image or facade.

We can respond to this process by restoring lost signifieds and reacquiring the meaning of things. This type of cultural criticism and resistance depends not only on examining the meaningful basis for individual action, but on the recovery of previously abandoned or marginalized group contexts. Cultural criticism involves recontextualization and a return to authentic cultural forms through the discovery of lost signifieds which counteracts the superficial consumerist culture of postmodernism that privileges image, appearance, and disembodied signifiers.

— MARK GOTTDIENER, *Postmodern Semiotics: Material Culture and the Forms of Postmodern Life* (Cambridge, Mass.: Blackwell, 1995), 233–34.

Earlier I quoted a passage from Saussure about the way concepts acquire meaning—by being what other concepts are not. And I mentioned that he defines a sign as a combination of a signifier (sound-object) and a signified (concept). It is crucial to remember, Saussure points out, that the relationship that exists between the signifier and the signified is arbitrary, based on convention, and not natural. This means that we must learn how to interpret signifiers and that the meaning of signifieds can change over time, as our conventions change.

This article is a bit technical, but the main point Gottdiener makes is that the culture industry tries to liberate signifiers from their traditional signifieds to use these debased signifiers in the service of creating hyperreal consumer cultures (think here of advertising and the mass media). Postmodernists are complicit in this activity, since postmodernism does not consider authenticity to be of any importance. The authentic meaning of signifiers is of little concern to them. What cultural critics must do, Gottdiener argues, is to find ways to reclaim the lost signifiers and regain a true understanding of the meanings of things, countering the postmodernist stress on images, appearances, and "disembodied" signifiers—that is, signs whose signifiers have been torn away from their traditional meanings in the service of consumer culture.

37

"Conservative" and "Critical" Postmodernism

"Postmodernism" has developed a bad reputation in communication research circles. It is often dismissed as lacking in responsibility and seriousness, as irresponsible and indifferent towards truth, justice, and other morally respectable modern goals. For many communication researchers who consider themselves the guardians of accountable scholarship, the postmodern raises the spectre of ideological vacuousness, stylistic excess, playful irreverence, and uncritical celebration of commercial culture, as well as an "anything goes" mentality, a nihilistic relativism when it comes to tried-and-tested values, standards and forms of knowledge. But this is a one-sided, and often facile, dismissal and characterization of the postmodern which, ironically, underestimates the seriousness an consequentiality of the so-called "postmodern condition."

At the very least, a distinction needs to be made between conservative and critical postmodernism as an intellectual attitude . . . while the former does indeed succumb to an "anything goes" attitude (and therefore indulges in a happy surrender to the seductions of postmodern culture), I would argue that the latter, postmodernism, is motivated by a deep understanding of the limits and failures of what Habermas calls the "unfinished project of modernity," by the need to respond to these limits and failures not through a forced extension of modernist ways of thinking, but through a sceptical questioning of the certainties and absolutisms of those ways of thinking. In this regard, the distinction between post-modern*ism* and postmodern*ity* is an important one: while one can refuse to be a postmodernist and remain loyal to the more secure convictions of modernism instead, one cannot, to all intents and purposes, deny or escape the reality of post-modernity, which as an over-all term, describes some of the social, political and cultural quandaries of the current world-historical condition. As Zygmunt Bauman . . . rather dramatically puts it, postmodernity is modernity coming of age, modernity coming to terms with its own impossibility: "Postmodernity is no more (but no less either) than the modern mind taking a long, attentive and sober look at itself, at its condition and its past works, not fully liking what it sees and sensing the urge to change." The critical postmodern sensibility, in short, is a response to the failure of modernity to live up to its own ideals and ambitions (including those of "progress" towards a more "just and decent society"), not by discarding those ideals and ambitions altogether but by recognizing and accepting the profound ambivalence involved in their pursuit.

— IEN ANG, "The Performance of the Sponge: Mass Communication Theory Enters the Postmodern World," in *The Media in Question: Popular Cultures and Public Interests,* ed. Kees Brants, Joke Hermes, and Liesbet van Zoonen (Thousand Oaks, Calif.: Sage, 1998), 77–78.

Ang makes a distinction between what she calls "conservative postmodernism" and "critical postmodernism." It is conservative postmodernism, she says, that has been attacked, and rightly so, she suggests, for being irreverent and having an "anything goes" perspective on things. On the other hand, critical postmodernism is serious and is involved with taking the ideals of modernism, especially the belief in progress toward a more just society, and trying to realize them. She also makes a distinction between postmodernism and postmodernity, arguing that we live in a postmodernist society and must realize that such is the case, but rather than just drifting along with the cultural tide, so to speak, we must adopt a critical perspective and do what we can to create a more just society. Critical communications scholars, I should point out, are primarily interested in the role communication plays in the social and political order, in contrast to administrative communications scholars, who are interested in analyzing communication and understanding it better, often in the service, ultimately, of governmental agencies or corporations.

38 ▸ Advertising, Women, and Postmodernism

Socialization theory teaches us that differences between men and women are produced by cultural variation and not by nature, while conversational analysis shows the differences in male and female patterns of conversational interruptions. However, as analyses of Western female culture, these are still rather superficial. We need a "thicker description." Here postmodernism, but this time of Baudrillard's brand, could prove to be significant. Apart from acting as a critic of modernity, postmodernism has a message of its own. The message is that the media are the message. Reality vanishes in an endless spiral of simulacra.... Landscapes are replaced by mediascapes. The body is invaded by signs written on it by the restless forces of advertising and publicity, which present us with selves we can or cannot present in everyday life. When he died Erving Goffman left an important heritage in *Gender Advertisements* (1979). That analysis revolves around the signs and symbols of (male) dominance and (female) submission.

Goffman showed us how women in relation to men have been depicted in inferior and/or child-like positions.... Goffman knew and warned us that advertisements are not reality. Nevertheless, he suggested that ads told us something about real life. The presentation of self to a certain extent is always the presentation of gender. This representation can be reduced merely to the use of power, but the implication could also be more subtle. For example, even in organizations where men and women are used to working together, certain power struggles, even when fought out in the presence of female colleagues, specifically belong to male cultures, like the telling of crude jokes or heavy teasing before the start of actual negotiations. Participation in this kind of impression management is taboo for the women. How to deal, for example, with men who show their power by leaning backwards in a chair with their thumbs in their armpit? What should women do if they want or have to portray similar shows of power? And what could be the female equivalent to crude joking or heavy teasing? Thus, women entering a masculine world both suffer from, and cause something of, a culture shock. Although it is less obvious, this discomfort also can be experienced by men when they enter the world of women. When approaching gender differences from this point of view, emancipation means getting to know the other's culture as well as learning how to transgress its borders in a civilized way. Emancipation means communication; it does not necessarily mean identification.

Apart from these interactional transgressions of boundaries, postmodernism teaches us how to play subversive games with traditional codes. In Canada, a perfume factory recently published an ad which showed a woman in her bloomers embracing a man from behind. In the Netherlands, van Gils, a producer of suits, advertises a naked boy in the arms of a fully dressed woman wearing a man's suit. . . . We could regard advertising these disjunctions as sign crimes, namely the endowing of a woman with the attributes of the phallocentric man from the fifties.

> — LIETEKE VAN VUCHT TIJSSEN, "Women between Modernity
> and Postmodernity," in *Theories of Modernity and Postmodernity*,
> ed. Bryan S. Turner (London: Sage, 1990), 160–61.

One of postmodernism's good points, some feminists argue, is the way it counters the dominant roles of males in societies, since postmodernism breaks down boundaries and attacks many "grand narratives" that have led to the dominance of men and the submission of women in most societies. There is another side to the story, though. Postmodernism is integrally tied to the mass media, to the endless succession of signs that film and television and photography generate.

The term "sign" can be taken in two different senses. In the first, I am using it the way Saussure did—as anything that can be used to represent something else, as a unification of signifier and a signified, whose meaning is based on convention. The second meaning of sign is a literal one—something used to sell something. Thus, if we look at the world of advertising, we find, as Goffman (1979) showed so convincingly, that advertising in all media is filled with images of dominant males and submissive females. Thus, it can be argued that what postmodernism gives to women with one hand, it takes away with the other. But, then, postmodernists don't place a high valuation on consistency.

Fragmentation. The splitting up of what used to be simpler and more mass-oriented, exemplified by the ever-growing product ranges and brand extensions in more and more specialized variations. Even within the retailing environment we experience the proliferation of outlets within the concentration of bigger outlets (shopping malls). Such specialized and stylized outlets often carry an in-depth assortment of a very narrow product range, such as teas or ties. The advertising media have also become fragmented, with more and more specialized TV channels, magazines, radio stations and websites for placing one's advertising.

De-differentiation. Postmodernists are interested in the blurring of distinctions between hierarchies such as "high and low culture," or politics and show business. Examples would be the use of artistic works in advertising and the celebration of advertising as artistic works. Companies such as Coca-Cola, Nike and Guinness have their own museums. Another clear example is the blurring of advertisements and TV programmes, wherein more and more TV programmes feature advertising for themselves (in order to increase viewer ratings) and TV commercials look like "real" programming. as in the ongoing soap opera with a couple spun around the coffee brand Gold Blend. The blurring of gender categories also refers to this aspect of postmodernism.

Hyperreality. The spreading of simulations and the loss of the sense of the "real" and the "authentic," as in the cases of re-engineered environments ... or in shopping centres simulating ancient Rome (The Forum in Las Vegas) or a Parisian street (West Edmonton Mall, Canada). Finally, products can be hyperreal to the extent that they simulate something else; for instance, sugarless sugar, fat-free-fat (olestra) or the butter replacement brand "I Can't Believe It's Not Butter." In fact, it has been argued that marketing may be the most important contributor to the creation of hyperreality, since the essence of marketing and particularly advertising is to create simulated reality by resignifying words, situations and brands.

Chronology. This refers to the consumer's search for the authentic and a preoccupation with the past—like real or authentic Chinese or Italian foods or the search for one's nostalgic roots in foods (or other consumer goods) as we "used to know it."

Pastiche. The playful and ironic mixing of existing categories and styles is typical of pastiche. An example would be one advertisement doing a parody of another or making references to slogans or other elements borrowed from other campaigns. Pastiche also involves self-referentiality (i.e. the advertisement recognizes itself as being an ad, by showing (mock) scenes from its own creative process).... [O]ther pastiches flourish, as when we see deliberate blurring of styles such as advertisements borrowing from films, or films and TV programmes borrowing from the advertisement style, all of it done "tongue-in-cheek."

Anti-Foundationalism. This last feature of postmodern marketing efforts refers not to parody but to an outright "anti-campaign campaign"— for example campaigns encouraging the receiver of the message *not* to take notice of the message since somebody is trying to seduce and take advantage of him or her.

— GARY BARMOSSY, SOREN ASKEGAARD, and MICHAEL SOLOMON, *Consumer Behaviour: A European Perspective* (Harrow, UK: Financial Times/Prentice Hall, 2002), 560–63.

On the basis of articles by various researchers who have done work on the impact of postmodernism on consumer behavior, our authors list six key features of postmodernism as it relates to marketing. These are fragmentation, dedifferentiation, hyperreality, chronology, pastiche, and antifoundationalism. One or more of these elements can be found in many contemporary advertising campaigns. If people have a postmodernist sensibility, it only makes sense to create advertising campaigns, in print and electronic media, that resonate with this sensibility. This is done by reflecting and using various characteristics of postmodernism.

Thus, we find hyperspecialization or fragmentation in many shopping malls, where stores often only carry one product range, such as teas, and we find dedifferentiation in some television campaigns where it becomes difficult to separate the commercials from the programs. The authors point out that marketing may be one of the main contributors to the development of hyperreality since the main purpose of advertising is to create a simulated reality. Pastiche, they suggest, involves the blending and mixing of categories and self-referentiality—referring to oneself—which might take the form of an advertisement pointing out that it is an advertisement or dealing with the process of its own creation. Chronology makes use of the anxiety of people in our rapidly changing postmodern societies by, among other things, using nostalgia and returning to the past, when life was simpler and easier to understand.

The postmodernist sensibility, which is ironic and skeptical, may also be teaching people to see through advertising and recognize it for what it is, hype. Another irony is that even though people see through it, they are still affected by it, which means that people are manipulated (if that's the correct word) by advertisements that they realize are trying to manipulate them. Postmodernism also seems to have a role in aestheticizing everyday life; it makes people more involved with style and design, helping them turn their lives into works of art, so to speak. Whether postmodernism is liberating people by helping them recognize the tricks advertising agencies are playing or helping them turn their lives into works of art, it is playing a larger and larger role in the strategizing of marketers and advertisers.

40 Postmodernism as an Attempt to Rescue Modernism

Posmodernist philosophers have rejected the notion of the unified subject of knowledge which characterized modernist thought. Following a tradition dating back to Nietzsche at least, they have attacked essentialist conceptions of human nature and human beings. Embodied as human beings are in culture and linguistic practices, the idea of the universal human subject can only be a fiction. As Foucault put it:

> From within language experienced and traversed as language, in the play of its possibilities extended to their furthest point, what emerges is that man has come to an end, and that, by reaching the summit of all possible speech. He arrives not only at the heart of himself but at the brink of that which limits him, in that region where death prowls, where thought is extinguished, where the promise of the origin interminably recedes.

Foucault emphasized that man, or woman, is the product of historically specific discourses. Critical analysis of these discourses can help us to dissolve the concept of man and of human nature and replace it by subjectivity understood in its social and historical context. He identified ethnology and psychology as the two disciplines which helped deconstruct the *category* man by drawing attention to cultural over-determination and the unconscious. The subject, his reason and desires and his consciousness should be understood as culturally produced.

The rejection of any notion of objective and universal truth and the authority of particular narratives claiming to represent truth has provided the basis for the attack on the grand narratives of the French and British Enlightenment. The notions of progress, universality and freedom, and a collective emancipatory project to attain them, which were found in the writings of philosophers of the Enlightenment have been targets of attack. The end of history has been proclaimed along with the dissolution of man. Instead, it is held, we should learn to listen to the voices which were submerged by the grand narratives, whether they be the voices of the colonial subjects or of women or any other marginalised group. This has revived interest in the everyday culture of different groups as expressed in the routines and rituals of their lives as also in the multiple, decentered struggles which are waged by people against the power which may be embodied in such practices.

Culture is indeed a primary concept for postmodernist philosophers, given their views on the social character of language and its role in mediating our experience of the world. They describe all human activity which produces mean-

80

ing as an expression of culture. However, the emphasis has been on engaging with culture rather than trying to look at it objectively from the outside, on interrogating it rather than accepting it as a framework of meaning which can only be interpreted to enable us to understand individual and collective action. Foucault and Derrida have drawn attention to the interconnection between power, cultural practices and social meanings. The role of radical cultural studies then would be to decode those discourses and try to subvert them.

— SARAH JOSEPH, *Interrogating Culture: Critical Perspectives onContemporary Social Theory* (New Delhi: Sage, 1998), 40–41.

Sarah Joseph returns to one of the basic aspects of postmodernist thought, its rejection of the notion that there are objective and universal truths based on the acceptance of grand narratives. This is connected with the notion that there is such a thing as an "essential" thing called human nature. There are only human beings, and they vary a great deal, with little in common at the cultural level. She quotes Michel Foucault, the French postmodernist, to the effect that "man has come to an end." We are all, Foucault suggests, the product of different histories, and to best understand humankind, we must consider the enormous variations in culture and subcultures that exist in any given society.

What the grand narratives did, Joseph suggests, was submerge the voices of colonial and marginal groups. With the rejection of modernism and its grand narratives, its belief in objective and universal truths, we now are beginning to hear the voices of the oppressed, of women, of minorities, and of others who have a great deal to offer to our understanding of societies and culture.

Joseph writes as a radical critical theorist, who asks us to consider the relationship that exists between power and cultural practices. What radical cultural studies must do is examine and decode the discourses of the powerful and try to subvert them. That, to a large degree, is what the postmodernist thinkers have tried to do. Marxists argue that their role is to expose the ideology of those who control societies, the ruling classes, and counter the hegemonic (all-embracing) ideological domination of societies by these ruling classes. From this perspective, postmodernism has a radical aspect to it.

Jenny Jones:

Boy, we have a show for you today! Recently, the University of Virginia philosopher Richard Rorty made the stunning declaration that nobody has "the foggiest idea" what postmodernism means. "It would be nice to get rid of it," he said. "It isn't exactly an idea; it's a word that pretends to stand for an idea."

Today we have with us a writer—a recovering postmodernist—who believes that his literary career and personal life have been irreparably damaged by the theory.... He wishes to remain anonymous, so we'll call him "Alex."

Alex, as an adolescent, before you began experimenting with postmodernism, you considered yourself—what?

Alex (his voice electronically altered):

A high modernist. Y'know, Pound, Eliot, Georges Braque, Wallace Stevens, Arnold Schoenberg, Mies van der Rohe. I had all of Schoenberg's 78's.

Jenny Jones:

And then you started reading people like Jean-François Lyotard and Jean Baudrillard—how did that change your feelings about your modernist heroes?

Alex:

I suddenly felt that they were, like, stifling and canonical.

Jenny Jones:

How old were you when you first read Fredric Jameson?

Alex:

Nine, I think. We used to go to a friend's house after school—y'know, his parents were never home—and we'd read, like, Paul Virilio and Julia Kristeva.

Jenny Jones:

So you're only 14, and you're already skeptical toward the "grand narratives" of modernity, you're questioning any belief system that claims universality or transcendence. And do you remember how you felt the very first time you entertained the notion that you and your universe are constituted by language—that reality is a cultural construct, a "text" whose meaning is determined by infinite associations with other "texts"?

Alex:

Uh, it felt, like, good.

Jenny Jones:

You're the child of a mixed marriage—is that right? Do you think that growing up in a mixed marriage made you more vulnerable to the siren song of postmodernism?

Alex:

Absolutely. It's hard when you're a little kid not to be able to just come right out and say (sniffles), y'know, I'm an Imagist or I'm a phenomenologist or I'm a post-painterly abstractionist. It's really hard especially around the holidays.

Jenny Jones:

Tell us how you think postmodernism affected your career as a novelist.

Alex:

I disavowed writing that contained real ideas or any real passion. My work became disjunctive, facetious and nihilistic. It was all blank parody, irony enveloped in more irony. It merely recapitulated the pernicious banality of television and advertising. I found myself indiscriminately incorporating any and all kinds of pop kitsch and shlock.

Jenny Jones:

And this spilled over into your personal life?

Alex:

It was impossible for me to experience life with any emotional intensity. I couldn't control the irony anymore. I perceived my own feelings as if they were in quotes. I italicized everything and everyone. It became impossible for me to appraise the quality of anything. To me everything was equivalent—the Brandenburg Concertos and the Lysol jingle had the same value.

> — MARK LEYNER, "Jenny Jones Interviews a Postmodernist," amster-dam.nettime.org/Lists_Archives/nettime+9807/msg00026.html [accessed November 21, 2002].

We have here a parody of the talk show format and a satire on postmodernism. If you are not familiar with postmodernist writers and the basic concepts connected with postmodernism, the satire will not have as much bite as if you are. Thus, the unnamed hero of this interview changes from a "high modernist" in his youth who liked T. S. Eliot and other modernist authors, musicians, and architects to a postmodernist who reads Lyotard and Baudrillard. He was nine when he first read Fredric Jameson. In the best postmodernist tradition, our hero sees no difference between a Bach masterpiece and a Lysol jingle. The interview manages to ridicule many of the basic concepts of postmodernism by creating a zany postmodernist character. It uses humor to render postmodernism absurd—or, as some would say, even more absurd than it already is.

Blade Runner **as a Postmodernist Film**

Many critics have cited *Blade Runner* as a postmodernist film. Some would argue that all Hollywood films are inherently postmodern, in that they generally recycle earlier forms of popular culture, such as comic books or gangster novels (*Batman*, *Pulp Fiction* etc.). Indeed, they can sometimes go so far as to recycle themselves, as the five *Rocky* films demonstrate. The difference, I believe, is that whilst most popular cinema is postmodern by virtue of existence, *Blade Runner* is consciously postmodern, in that it explores some of the issues the phrase relates to.

Postmodernism is a word that refers to many things, not least of them being a reference to the ways that signs become more important than the things they signify. . . . The idea of the 'simulacra' lies at the heart of *Blade Runner.* The simulacra of the film, replicants, are indistinguishable from humans. 'Human' is a very ambiguous term. Structuralism dictates that it is the relationships between elements of the code that give it signification. The word 'human' requires a context, in this case, 'replicant', to give it meaning— by juxtaposing ourselves in binary opposition with another we define ourselves. This sheds light on many aspects of the film. Why are the replicants not allowed on Earth? Why, if they are capable of developing their own emotional responses, are they ruthlessly denied the opportunity to do so? The answer to these questions relates directly to the Human/Replicant relationship. The humans of the film treat the replicants ruthlessly because, in a way, they must, in order to give the concept of human meaning in the postmodern world. But they cannot keep this violent hierarchy from collapsing; the replicants prove they can be just as human as the humans themselves. The cultural code upon which the world of the film is based is, like the city itself, corroding, resulting in a crisis of definition for humanity. . . .

Pastiche is perhaps the favourite form of postmodernists: the best example of this would be Andy Warhol's painting *Thirty are better than one.* *Blade Runner* itself engages in pastiche on more than one level. First, its architecture reveals several different styles. The first few shots of the film show futuristic looking refineries, but then concentrate on a futuristic building that is a pastiche of Mayan architecture. The interiors of the Tyrell Corporation that are shown, however, are designed in an Establishment Gothic look. The police headquarters of the film was designed to echo the Art Deco look of the Chrysler Building, in New York City, and the Bradbury Building, in which the final chase scene of the film is set, is an architectural anomaly, built in 1883 by an architect heavily influenced by a utopian book he had read about the year 2000. Animoid Row, where Deckard goes to discover the origins of the snake scale, seems to resemble a Middle Eastern bazaar. *Blade Runner*'s presentation of Los Angeles in 2019 as a postmodern architectural *entrepot* accentuates the ahistorical nature of postmodernist art.

— MAJID SALIM, "A Study of Ridley Scott's *Blade Runner*," www.majid-salim.co.uk/br/pa.html [accessed February 6, 2002].

*B*lade Runner, we are told, is a quintessentially postmodernist film in that it is consciously postmodern, unlike many other films that may have postmodern elements but are accidentally postmodern, so to speak. For one thing, it explores the complicated relationship between simulations and reality. In the film, this relationship takes the form of the conflict between replicants (the simulations) and human beings (the real thing).

What replicants don't have, we are told, is a sense of history—because they have no history, having been manufactured to do certain things. But the replicants look exactly like human beings and behave like them, except, of course, that they are not human. The humans treat replicants the way they do, in part, as a means of affirming their humanity. This makes sense if we recall Saussure's notion that concepts are only defined differentially, that nothing makes sense in itself. So replicants enable humans to define themselves as human. In essence, being human means not being a replicant, though if you look at a replicant, you can't tell that it isn't human. That is one of the problems replicants pose to humans—their otherness is not visually evident.

In addition, stylistically the film reflects postmodernist themes, especially the notion of pastiche—for the Los Angeles of 2019 in which the film takes place is a hodgepodge of different architectural styles, and the director, Ridley Scott, uses certain buildings consciously in an effort to suggest a world in which stylistic eclecticism in architecture and everyday life is the rule.

43 Postmodernism and the Postmodern Novel

Few terms have been subject to such intense debates as "postmodernism." Though its indiscriminate use has all but exhausted the word of any kind of precise meaning, one can distinguish three major usages: (i) to refer to the non-realist and non-traditional literature and art of the post-World War Two period; (ii) to refer to literature and art which takes certain characteristics to an extreme stage . . . ; and (iii) to refer to a more general human condition in the "late-capitalist" world of the post 1950s, a period marked by the end of what Jean-François Lyotard calls the grand "meta-narratives" of western culture. The myths by which we once legitimized knowledge and practice—Christianity, Science, Democracy, Communism, Progress—no longer have the unquestioning support necessary to sustain the projects which were undertaken in their name, resulting in a radical modification of our cultural sphere. It is not simply that postmodernism does not believe in "truth" so much as that it understands truth and meaning as historically constructed and thus seeks to expose the mechanisms by which this production is hidden and "naturalized."

Among the modernist devices which postmodernism pushes to a new extreme are: the rejection of mimetic representation in favour of a self-referential "playing" with the forms, conventions and icons of "high art" and literature; the rejection of the cult of originality in recognition of the inevitable loss of origin in the age of mass production; the rejection of plot and character as meaningful artistic conventions; and the rejection of meaning itself as delusory.

However, where modernism thought of itself as a last ditch attempt to shore up, like Eliot's Fisher King, the ruins of western culture, postmodernists often gleefully accept its demise and plunder its remains for their artistic materials. Andy Warhol's multiple images of Marilyn Monroe and Kathy Acker's re-writing of Cervantes' *Don Quixote* are representative of the postmodernist trend toward *bricolage,* the use of the bits and pieces of older artifacts to produce a new, if not "original," work of art, a work which blurs the traditional distinctions between the old and the new even as it blurs those between high and low art.

Postmodernism in literature is usually associated with (among others) Acker, Barth, Thomas Pynchon, Donald Bartheleme, Jorge Luis Borges, Italo Calvino and John Ashberry. Their literary strategies widely differ, but each shows a self-reflexive interest in the processes of narrative itself and the means by which it constructs both text and reader. . . .

Though postmodernism is considered something of a spent force in certain circles ... its legacy is perhaps the most dominant context for the formal experimentation which characterizes it. If postmodernism is condemned for having given up the world of social and political engagement for the solipsistic pleasures of word play, what will be said of a fiction that entices its readers into the ethereal void of the electronic word?

— CHRISTOPHER KEEP, TIM MCLAUGHLIN, and ROBIN PARMAR,
"Postmodernism and the Postmodern Novel,"
www.iath.virginia.edu/elab/hflo256.html [accessed June 6, 2002].

Our authors deal with some of the basic devices used by postmodernist writers, such as a lack of concern with plot, character, and originality; a fascination with identity, images, and copies of things; and a playful approach to, and subversion of, various modernist conventions. Quite clearly, we have a different sensibility with postmodern writers. For example, Italo Calvino subverts the traditional narrative line in his novel *If on a Winter's Night a Traveler* and offers a collection of what can be construed as first chapters for a number of different novels that all fit together, somehow, in the end, into a novel.

David Lodge, in his book *The Modes of Modern Writing: Metaphor, Metonymy, and the Typology of Modern Literature (1997),* suggests that postmodern literature has five basic techniques: contradiction, permutation, discontinuity, randomness, and excess. It is difficult to take as complex a phenomenon as postmodernism and reduce its impact on literature to five techniques, but Lodge's formulation gives a good overview of some of the more important characteristics of postmodernist literature, and we can find many of these techniques in the works of postmodernist writers. We find these techniques in Calvino's novels, Borges's stories, Perec's works, and the works of other postmodernist writers. It is probably the case that these techniques contribute to the fascination, and in some cases puzzlement, we feel about their works.

In "Signs, Symbols and Discourses: A New Direction for Computer-Aided Literary Studies," Mark Olsen argues that "three decades of literary computing have failed to have any substantial impact on the mainstream of literary criticism and scholarship." ... One computing services expert, speaking about how the exciting growth of the internet has quickened the pace of academic exchange, innocently comments that it is like having a television with a million channels—"with that many channels, you could see all the television that has ever been done ... ; you could see anything you wanted, anytime, all the time." As critics often point out, there is something fast food–like about this increased access to and increase of information, something amounting to, to use Ian Lancashire's phrase, a "McDonaldization of knowledge."

What these analogies intriguingly suggest is just how closely tied technology is to an aesthetics of pastiche. Critical work on hypertext has tended to focus largely on hypertext fiction or on the more general concept of hypertext as an infinitely expandable set of linked documents or lexia, rather than on the suitability of hypertext for publishing scholarly material. In this paper I want to explore the relationship between the discourse of pastiche as a genre and the discourse of critical work on hypertext in order to examine assumptions about hypertextual scholarship. Powerful value associations colour this issue of "suitability", associations that may be grounded as firmly in aesthetics as in a reaction to the technology itself. My argument consists of two sections, the first linking definitions of pastiche to hypertext webs and the second concentrating more specifically on pastiche and hypertext as value-laden communication processes.

The word "pastiche", derived from the Italian for "pie" or "pastry", is defined in the *OED* as "a jumble", "a medley of various ingredients", "a potpourri", or "a design made up of fragments pieced together or copied with modification from an original". The term applies well to electronic projects that combine a variety of media, such as text, graphics, audio clips, and video clips. The term would also seem to apply well to the range of materials—from course listings and syllabi to pointers to other relevant sites—found on the text-only versions of many literary studies webs, as well as to electronic articles and fiction whose use of hypertext's referential characteristics compartmentalizes the material into a non-linear collection of linked lexia. Significantly, the term "pastiche" has undergone a progressively more negative valuation, particularly in the ways it has been distinguished from parody, and in the so-called critiques of postmodernism delivered by Lyotard, Baudrillard, and Jameson, as well as in the works of Derrida and Hutcheon.

— ANDREA AUSTIN, "Notes on the Collision between Humanities Scholarship and Hypertext: Virtuality Rewarded," *TEXT Technology* 6, no. 3 (1996), www.chass.utoronto.ca/epc.chwp/austin [accessedMarch 6, 2002].

There is, the author of this essay suggests, a significant relationship between hypertext and pastiche. There are similarities between technology's nonlinearity and the aesthetic of the pastiche, which she defines as fragments pieced together, often with modifications by the person making the pastiche. Artists who use electronic media invariably find themselves patching together bits and pieces of this and that, which they've taken from elsewhere—in other words, making pastiches. She concludes this selection by pointing out that postmodernists have given the pastiche an increasingly negative valuation. We saw this in the second essay in this book, in which Fredric Jameson criticizes the pastiche as being neutral and not having the satiric content of the parody.

45 The Flavors of Postmodernity

Fusion cuisine is postmodern. Its "vivid colors and cross-cultural style" (as characterized by the publisher's dust jacket text to Hugh Carpenter and Teri Sandison's *Fusion Food Cookbook*) reflect its "fusion" of elements from different (and often culturally opposed) traditions. The consciously created results illustrate the dynamic interreferentiality that characterizes the postmodern in various art forms. As such, fusion cuisine offers a site for interrogating the promises and contradictions of postmodern theory. Like Charles Jencks's exploration of the postmodern in architecture, I propose to examine a concrete postmodern practice as a context in which to understand the otherwise abstract claims of postmodern theory.

Noting that the term was invented by Norman Van Aiken (of Norman's in Miami), Andrew Dornenburg and Karen Page define fusion cuisine as "a harmonious combination of foods of various origins, popularized at restaurants ranging from Lydia Shore's restaurant Biba (Boston) to Susan Finiger and Mary Sue Milliken's City Restaurant (Los Angeles)." They also provide the more precise industry definition which restricts fusion to "a melding of ingredients and/or techniques of two or more regions" in a single dish; they use the term "eclectic" to refer to mixing regional influences across courses or in a menu. They attribute the force behind the spread of fusion cuisine to shifting demographics; increasingly diverse populations both introduce new traditions and provide an audience for reinterpretations of those traditions....

Pound's famous modernist injunction to "make it new" can be seen in food culture in two parallel trends: nouvelle cuisine and highly refined ethnic cuisines. The first made classical French cuisine new by reducing the complicated flavors of traditional preparations to seemingly simple, intense essences; the now comic stereotype of the nouvelle cuisine's small portions also reveals its emphasis on few, distinct flavors abstracted from the sheer substance of traditional French cookery. The second can be seen as making other foodways new by applying the ethos of nouvelle cuisine to food traditions outside the dominant sphere of French cookery; the search for the "essence" of specific foodways led to the rejection of "inauthentic" methods and ingredients in an attempt to recreate "pure" cuisines.

If both these trends illustrate the modernist urge to make the familiar new, they also reflect the modernist problem of enacting a separation between art and everyday life. With nouvelle cuisine, the emphasis on flavor over—even to the exclusion of—substance replaced the traditional utilitarianism of food, thus limiting its appeal to a small, highly affluent subculture;

with refined ethnic cuisine, the emphasis on authenticity excluded those with untrained (or at least inexperienced) palates, thus limiting its appeal to those, again mostly affluent, with the time and money to cultivate appreciation for "foreign" tastes.

Fusion cuisine, on the other hand, reflects "the determination of post-modernism's champions to pull art back into the maelstrom of daily life." . . . Its diversity of tastes reflects its diversity of influences. Here fusion dares to combine traditions previously believed relentlessly incompatible.

— MARK McWILLIAMS, www.people.virginia.edu/~mbmsw/papers/ fusion.html [accessed March 18, 2002].

Thanks to this article by Mark McWilliams, which was presented at a conference at the University of Virginia, "The Flavors of Postmodernity," we can now understand the development of fusion food restaurants and the popularity of these fusion foods with their patrons. The creation of these dishes came about because chefs developed a new sensibility—what can be called a postmodern sensibility—as far as food is concerned. And just as postmodernism is identified with double coding in architecture and the pastiche in literary works, postmodernism manifests itself, on the restaurant scene, as fusion food.

Fusion food involves blending two or more distinctive cuisines—such as Japanese and French or Italian and Chinese or French and Mexican or Japanese and Mexican. One could go on endlessly here. What is important is that cuisines that before the development of fusion foods were thought to be incompatible suddenly were fused together, creating some remarkable new dishes with strange new tastes. The barriers between popular culture and elite culture were broken by the postmodernists, and so were the barriers between so-called distinctive cuisines, resulting in fusion cuisine.

I quoted Lyotard earlier on the matter of eclecticism as the "degree zero" of contemporary culture. But after listening to reggae in one's retro clothes and watching a western, it is even more "postmodernist," I would suggest, to have a fusion lunch in a postmodern building than to eat a McDonald's hamburger.

What do the following have in common?

A poem about the characters in a book, and about the reader of that book, and about what they are doing when the book is not being read. [The poem, "Reading in Place," is in Mark Strand's collection *The Continuous Life* (1990).]

An American television series combining the elements of a murder mystery, a soap opera, a parody of a murder mystery, and a parody of a soap opera, in which the expected generic conventions occur but ironically, everything happening as if between invisible quotation marks. [The series is *Twin Peaks* by David Lynch (1990).]

A British television series in which a hardboiled detective plot—long on wisecracks, tough talk, trenchcoats, and mean streets—is systematically punctuated by the crooning of romantic tunes from the 1940s. The incongruousness of the juxtaposition is calculated, dramatizing that the cynical detective is in fact a disillusioned romantic in the Sinatra manner. [The series is *The Singing Detective* by Dennis Potter (1986).]

A story whose characters include the pieces on a board game as well as the people who manipulate them. What is the inner life of Colonel Mustard? Miss Scarlet? Professor Plum? [The story is "A Game of Clue" from Steven Millhauser's book *The Barnum Museum* (1990).]

A book of sestinas about Perry Mason, Della Street, Paul Drake, Hamilton Burger, and Lieutenant Tragg. [The book is *The Whole Truth* by James Cummins (1986).]

A novel about the adventures of a feline character from a once beloved, now defunct comic strip, who gets to be psychoanalyzed, witnesses the development of the atomic bomb, and speaks in a punning idiolect in which "capitalism" becomes "keepitallism," psychoanalysis "sighcowandallis," nuclear physics "newclear fizzsticks," and virus "whyrus." [The novel, based on George Herriman's comic strip of the same name, is *Krazy Kat* by Jay Cantor (1988).]

A novel about the lives of movie protagonists before and after the Hollywood films in which they figure. What happens to Rick Blaine after he and Captain Renault toast the beginning of their beautiful friendship at the end of *Casablanca?* What does George Bailey do with all the money he gets at the close of *It's a Wonderful Life?* What was Kay Corleone's childhood like, and how does she get along with her estranged son after her husband exiles her from the family in *The Godfather, Part II?* [The novel that answers these and other such questions is *Suspects* by David Thompson (1985).]

— DAVID LEHMAN, "The Questions of Postmodernism,"
www.zip.com.au/~jtranter/jacket04/lehman-postmod.html
[accessed June 6, 2002].

In this passage, taken from a long essay on postmodernism and contemporary culture, we get a sense of the way the postmodern sensibility plays with people and uses their knowledge and experiences for its own purposes. Thus, we find novels about characters from the funnies (*Krazy Kat*) and about characters from movies before they appeared in the movie and after the movie finished. We are, in short, dealing with a postmodern sensibility that recognizes no boundaries and feels free to do what it wants with characters created by other writers, cartoonists, or film directors.

Postmodernists also play with conventions in various genres and feels free to mix them up in any way they want. Thus, for example, *Twin Peaks* is described as a hodgepodge of different genres—which may explain its initial fascination for television viewers and their subsequent disillusionment with it. There is, I would suggest, a common thread in all of the works cited—a desire to play with conventions, a comedic perspective that, for example, enables writers to take characters created by others and continue with their lives in books they write.

47 **Postmodernism and Therapy: An Interview with Lois Shawver**

Who do you contrast with the postmoderns? Who is there, in other words, who is not postmodern?
I think there are three groups of people: the premoderns, the moderns, and the postmoderns. The premoderns are the people who explain things with literal parables such as people who take the Bible literally. The moderns, in contrast, try to put all their beliefs in scientific sounding theories. The postmoderns are more likely to take a non-literal but poetic approach to expressing themselves.

Do the postmoderns have a common set of beliefs?
Not really. They have different beliefs but they share a kind of humility about their beliefs. They treat their beliefs more like hunches than like faithful allegiances. They often describe themselves as "not-knowing" or "non-knowing". They take a professional stance without presenting themselves as experts. They offer help without presenting themselves as authorities. Although there are no real common beliefs, however, there is a common style of talking that frequently emerges from this shared skepticism.

Isn't it a loss not to have firm and committed beliefs?
Some people think so. I call these people "nostalgic postmoderns." I contrast them with the more "utopian" postmoderns. Utopian postmoderns have discovered something to replace their committed beliefs.

What replaces committed beliefs?
A special kind of conversation that I call "paralogy" after Jean-François Lyotard, one of the leaders of the postmodern movement. In paralogical conversations, people of quite diverse points of view, even modern or premodern points of view, find ways to talk together and make sense together. Instead of talking past each other or down to each other, they learn from each other, or that's what they try to do. Paralogy is a very satisfying, very alluring kind of conversation that sometimes happens when people of diverse views come together and listen to each other. Because they no longer feel so firmly committed to a package of ideas (a theory or a parable), they can sometimes listen to each other with more generosity, and learn more from each other. It is not that people begin to think the same so much as that conceptual shifts begin to happen. This can be very exciting. Each conversationalist becomes more creative, more visionary. Once the conversation becomes more creative, many people do not miss the paternalism of modern and premodern forms of life.

Where would I find postmodernism manifesting itself?
Everywhere in the western world where conversation is encouraged. Modernity was the culture of the book, but the book divides people into authors and readers. The authors and readers never meet each other. There is no conversation. Authors simply provide the ideas and readers simply drink them in. But in the postmodern culture, people are turning away from books and prefer conversational paralogy. They are tired of monologues. They want to talk with each other, or listen to others talk.

— "What Is Postmodernism and What Does It Have to Do with Therapy, Anyway? An Interview with Lois Shawver," www.newtherapist.com.lois6.html [accessed January 4, 2002].

Lois Shawver, the person being interviewed, has a website on postmodern therapy. She emphasizes the importance of paralogy, which can be contrasted with monology, where people talk with little concern for what others might want to say. It is important to learn how to listen to others so as to be able to converse with them, and it is also important to recognize that one doesn't necessarily have all the answers. Monologism was typical of modern and premodern cultures, where people talked past one another. In a postmodern culture, where paralogy is a cultural dominant, people recognize the value and importance of what others have to say, which leads, Shawver suggests, to a more creative kind of conversation—and therapy.

In modernist cultures, the author suggests, people had committed beliefs, which they championed. Thus, every conversation became a kind of argument with contending opponents, certain of the validity of their beliefs. In postmodernist cultures, where the paralogical mode of speaking is common, people are much more democratic and inclined to listen to others. They do not automatically reject ideas that are not congruent with their particular beliefs.

This suggests that postmodernism has democratic implications and that therapy is not a one-way street with all the wisdom coming from the therapist; postmodern therapy becomes much more creative because the therapist does not assume that he or she has all the answers.

48 ▶ Romantic Love in Postmodern Societies

Most traditional societies privilege comfort and carefully attempt to control (or suppress) the expression of the drive to excitation exemplified in sexual attraction. . . . [T]he cultural ideal of romantic love has given a greater legitimacy to the intensity of passion and sexual attraction as it emphasizes the uniqueness of the loved one and restricts the possible number of partners by subsuming the romantic biography under a single life-long narrative of love ("*le grand amour*"). But this narrative of love almost never becomes a narrative of comfort. Since it must affirm the supremacy of passion, it is usually doomed to end with the parting or death of the lovers. Postmodern romance has seen the collapse of overarching life-long romance narratives, which it has compressed into the briefer and repeatable form of the *affair*.

The "affair" is related to the transformations undergone by sexuality after the Second World War. . . . During this period, sex for its own sake was progressively legitimized and promoted by the political discourses of feminism and gay liberation, a process that was aided by the powerful cultural idioms of the sphere of consumption. In its intrinsic transience and affirmation of pleasure, novelty and excitement, the affair may be dubbed a postmodern experience and contains a structure of feeling with affinities to the emotions and cultural values fostered by the sphere of consumption.

As Scitovsky argues, consumption rests on the drive toward excitation because the purchase and experience of new commodities are a source of pleasure:

> Novelty is a major source of satisfaction, to judge by the large quantity we avidly consume every day and the high value we place on it. First love, first taste of some special food, or a naked body, today with many firsts, are among our most cherished memories. (T. Scitovsky, *The Joyless Economy*. 1976. New York: Oxford University Press.)

In contradistinction to the teleological, absolute, and single-minded Romantic narrative of "grand amour," the affair is a cultural form that attempts to immobilize and repeat, compulsively, the primordial experience of "novelty." During the Victorian era, people chose from a very narrow pool of available partners and often felt compelled to marry their first suitor. The contemporary affair, by contrast, presupposes variety and freedom to choose. This "shop-and-choose" outlook is due to a much wider pool of available partners and to the fact that a marketplace viewpoint—the belief that one should commit oneself after a long process of information gathering—has pervaded romantic practices. . . . The affair can be viewed as a postmodern expression of *intensities* or experiences of pure sensations, desire, pleasures, non-mediated by reason, language or a master narrative of self.

— EVA ILLOUZ, "The Lost Innocence of Love: Romance as a Postmodern Condition," *Theory, Culture, and Society* 15, nos. 3–4 (1998): 175–76.

Marriage, from the point of view of postmodernists, can be seen as one more narrative that we inherited from the modernists and from others who came before them. [One of the Ten Commandments, recall, tells us not to commit adultery.] You marry someone and live with them for the rest of your life. We learn about this from fairy tales, when princesses marry heroes and we are told "they lived happily ever after." Statistics show, alas, that this fantasy we all carry in our heads isn't realized that often. Something like half of all marriages now end in divorce. The traditional long-lasting marriage has been replaced by serial monogamy. Many divorced people marry again, and some of them get divorced again.

The postmodern perspective on romantic love is considerably different from the modernist one. Marriage and its narrative of fidelity have been replaced, in a consumerist culture, with the affair, an attempt, our author suggests, to relive the passion and emotional excitement we felt when we first had sex with someone. It is similar in nature to buying a new car—or anything new. Our desire for novelty and the sensations connected with purchasing or obtaining something new become fused with sex, so the affair offers the best of two worlds—the attractiveness of newness and the gratification of sexual pleasure, for both sexes. Sex has become one more lifestyle choice—an expression of autonomy not too far removed in nature from buying a pair of jeans.

Modernism and Postmodernism in the Arts

Postmodernism validates the nonintentional. It validates polytheism and a concern for the environment, ecology. Perhaps the first awareness of postmodernism was in the field of architecture. It is in architecture that the multifarious manifestations of postmodernism are most clearly visible.... In architecture, postmodernism is a comparative concept, as it is in general, and therefore it must be contrasted with modernism. Postmodernism is not the opposite of modernism, as it is often portrayed, but is rather broader, more inclusive, and encompasses modernism within it. Charles Jencks, perhaps the foremost spokeperson on postmodernism architecture, describes it as "double coding"; i.e., it is modern architecture with something else juxtaposed on it. This "something else" is not an amalgamation but must be contrasting, eclectic. This is often a historicist juxtaposition (something from the past), but may also be from a different culture; e.g., Western + Japanese, or a different aesthetic. As such, postmodernism seems to represent a period of transition, a period in which a uniform aesthetic has not yet matured.

Dates can only be artificial divisions, but they are useful as guidelines. Modern music is generally considered to be a period from about 1910 to 1960, with 1960–70 being a transitional stage. Modern composers include Schoenberg, Bartok, Varese, and Stravinsky. Postmodern composers include John Zorn, and Frank Zappa. But, Charles Ives was, in some ways, a proto-postmodernist who lived early in the century, which demonstrates that dates cannot be relied upon completely. On the other hand, modernism survives today as late-modernism, with such composers as Pierre Boulez, Milton Babbitt, and Karlheinz Stockhausen.

Modern artists include Piet Mondrian, Paul Klee, Joan Miró, Pablo Picasso, Willem de Kooning, and Mark Rothko. Postmodern artists include Peter Blake, Ron Kitaj, and Robert Longo. Postmodern architects include Charles Moore (Piazza d'Italia), Michael Graves (Portland Public Service Building), and Yasufumi Kijima (Matsuo Shrine). Modern science is represented by Einstein's relativity and unified field theories. Postmodern science includes quantum theory, indeterminacy, and chaos.

The following chart, garnered from various sources with some additions, is meant to contrast modernism with postmodernism, but any such chart is bound to be an oversimplified generalization. Nevertheless, distinctions are necessary and useful. This is offered as such. The contrasts between the two are rarely clear-cut, and postmodern thought normally embraces modernism within it.

Modern	Postmodern
monotheism, atheism	pantheism
authoritarian, totalitarian	democratic
utopian, elitist	populist
patriarchal	non-patriarchal, feminism
hierarchical	anarchical
totalization	non-totalized, fragmented
centered	dispersed
European, Western	global, multicultural
master code	idiolects
uniformity	diversity
determinist	indeterminant
objectivism	anthropic principle
objectivist values	values from nature
detached	participatory
separation from and control of nature	ecological, harmonious with nature
staid, serious	playful, ironic
formal	non-formal
purposeful	playful
intentional, constructive	non-intentional, deconstructive
progress	dynamics
theoretical	practical, pragmatic
reductive, analytic	synthetic
simplicity, elegance, spartan	elaboration
logical	spiritual
Newtonian mechanics, Relativity	quantum mechanics, chaos
cause-effect	synchronicity
control-design	chance
linear	multi-pathed
harmonious, integrated	eclectic, non-integrated
permanence	transience
abstraction	representation
material	semiotic
non-communicative	communicative
anti-symbolic	pro-symbolic
anti-metaphorical	pro-metaphorical
non-narrative	narrative
nonhistoricist, cult of the "new"	historicism
mechanical	electronic
analog	digital

— LARRY SOLOMON, "What Is Postmodernism?"
    azstarnet;.com/~solo/postmod.htm [accessed November 18, 2001].

L arry Solomon does a number of important things that help us understand postmodernism. Like many other writers on the subject, he lists some of the more important modernist and postmodernist artists, architects, composers, and musicians. This method, exemplification, is a helpful device to enable readers to get a better idea of what postmodernism is. Then, he does something even more useful—he offers us a valuable tool, a chart that offers a comparison that contrasts some of the most important elements of modernism and postmodernism. Charts like this are very useful in that they enable us to see the core ideas of movements such as modernism and postmodernism; they point out the differences, in a very graphic manner, between the two, though as Solomon explains, charts are always somewhat simplistic. This chart, like the one that follows in the next section, functions as a kind of summary of many of the topics discussed in this book.

Charts would seem to be modernist constructs, based on the notion that comparisons are necessary for concepts to have meaning—a notion we have already dealt with in the section on Ferdinand de Saussure's theories about semiotics.

Modernism/Modernity	Postmodern/Postmodernity
Master Narratives and Metanarratives of history, culture and national identity; myths of cultural and ethnic origin.	Suspicion and rejection of Master Narratives; local narratives, ironic deconstruction of master narratives; counter-myths of origin.
Faith in "Grand Theory" (totalizing explanations in history, science and culture) to represent all knowledge and explain everything.	Rejection of totalizing theories; pursuit of localizing and contingent theories.
Faith in, and myths of, social and cultural unity, hierarchies of social-class and ethnic/ national values, seemingly clear bases for unity.	Social and cultural pluralism, disunity, unclear bases for social/national/ethnic unity.
Master narrative of progress through science and technology.	Skepticism of progress, anti-technology reactions, neo-Luddism; new age religions.
Sense of unified, centered self; "individualism," unified identity.	Sense of fragmentation and decentered self; multiple, conflicting identities.
Idea of "the family" as central unit of social order; model of the middle-class, nuclear family.	Alternative family units, alternatives to middle-class marriage model; multiple identities for couplings and childraising.
Hierarchy, order, centralized control.	Subverted order, loss of centralized control, fragmentation.

Modernism/Modernity	Postmodern/Postmodernity
Faith and personal investment in big politics (Nation-State, party).	Trust and investment in micropolitics, identity politics, local politics, institutional power struggles.
Faith in "Depth" (meaning, value, content, the signified) over "Surface" (appearances, the superficial, the signifier).	Attention to play of surfaces, images, signifiers without concern for "Depth."
Faith in the "real" beyond media and representations; authenticity of "originals."	Hyper-reality, image saturation, simulacra seem more powerful than the "real"; images and texts with no prior "original." As seen on TV" and "as seen on MTV" are more powerful than unmediated experience.
Dichotomy of high and low culture (official vs. popular culture); imposed consensus that high or official culture is normative and authoritative.	Disruption of the dominance of high culture by popular culture; mixing of popular and high cultures, new valuation of pop culture, hybrid cultural forms cancel "high"/"low" categories.
Mass culture, mass consumption, mass marketing.	Demassified culture; niche products and marketing, smaller group identities.
Art as unique object and finished work authenticated by artist and validated by agreed upon standards.	Art as process, performance, production, intertextuality. Art as recycling of culture authenticated by audience and validated in subcultures sharing identity with the artist.
Knowledge mastery, attempts to embrace a totality.	Navigation, information management, just-in-time knowledge.
The encyclopedia.	The Web.

Modernism/Modernity	Postmodern/Postmodernity
Determinancy.	Indeterminancy, contingency.
Seriousness of intention and purpose, middle-class earnestness.	Play, irony, challenge to official seriousness, subversion of earnestness.
Sense of clear generic boundaries and wholeness (art, music, and literature).	Hybridity, promiscuous genres, recombinant culture, intertextuality, pastiche.
Design and architecture of New York and Boston.	Design and architecture of LA and Las Vegas.
Clear dichotomy between organic and inorganic, human and machine.	Cyborgian mixing of organic and inorganic, human and machine and electronic.
Phallic ordering of sexual difference, unified sexualities, exclusion/bracketing of pornography.	Androgyny, queer sexual identities, polymorphous sexuality, mass marketing of pornography.
The book as sufficient bearer of the word.	Hypermedia as transcendence of physical limits of print media.
The library as system for printed knowledge.	The Web or Net as information system.

— MARTIN IRVINE "The Postmodern, Postmodernism, Postmodernity: Approaches to Po-Mo," 1998, www.georgetown.edu/irvinemi/technoculture/pomo.html [accessed December 18, 2001].

This chart, like the one in the previous section, offers a comparison between modernism and postmodernism. This chart has the advantage of adding more details and of providing information about a number of subjects not included in the earlier one. Using the two charts, you should be able to understand better how the two movements differ and how their core beliefs affect their attitudes toward elite culture, popular culture, architecture, sexuality, the nature of art, hyperreality, books, the Web, the family, hierarchy, and so on.

We end as we began, with the rejection of grand narratives, with skepticism about the notion of progress (one of the most important or grandest of our metanarratives), with a view of the world as fragmented, full of illusions, full of images of questionable veracity—that is, a hyperreality rather than a reality we can know, in which the oppositions that we had taken for granted no longer are accepted. Texts no longer are seen as autonomous as we thought they were, since we realize now that they are all intertextually related to previous texts. The split between elite culture and popular culture is no longer accepted. We live, Irvine suggests, in a world of indeterminacy, hybridity, promiscuity, androgyny, and hyperreality in which the proper stance is irony. The encyclopedia has been replaced by the Web, which means we search for information that interests us and no longer are forced to rely on the authority of those who published printed encyclopedias. The postmodern world may be more unsettling than the modernist world it replaced, but it is, at the very least, much more exciting.

A Concluding Note

One of the things about postmodern novels is that not being concerned with narrative line, they are not terribly concerned with conclusions, and some postmodern novels, such as Pynchon's *Crying of Lot 49*, don't seem to have a conclusion—at least not one that literary critics and theorists are happy with. This book doesn't have a conclusion per se, but rather an ending that I have imposed upon it. If there are 150,000 websites that mention postmodernism, I could spend the rest of my life checking them out. And, no doubt, as I check out the sites, new ones would be added.

It turns out that the pastiche is the basic model, the pattern, the "script," the matrix, the code, the template, the "cultural dominant" (in Jameson's words) for postmodernist works of art and postmodernist culture—whether it be novels, buildings, films, shopping malls, or Disneylands. Once a culture has become postmodernist, our authors suggest, young people growing up in such a culture learn—from the media, from their friends, from everything they see around them—postmodern attitudes and beliefs. And whether they realize it or not, they adopt postmodernist practices.

Many people are leading postmodern lives who have never even heard the term. (This is not so remarkable, if you think about it. Paranoid schizophrenics may not realize what ailment they have and may never have heard the term, either. What we are is, in many cases, the result of what others—some of whom have expertise in one area or another—tell us we are.)

And so I leave you with the hope that the selections I have put together in this book, the pastiche I have created to explain postmodernism, helps you better understand what postmodernism is and how it has affected our culture and many areas of our day-to-day lives. At the very least, I hope you will understand what Lyotard meant when he wrote "simplifying to the extreme, I define postmodern as incredulity toward metanarratives."

References

Abian, K. Wilhelm. 2002. "Deconstructing Debord: Feminism and Subconstructive Theory."

Austin, Andrea. 1996. "Notes on the Collision between Humanities Scholarship and Hypertext: Virtuality Rewarded." *TEXT Technology* 6, no. 3. www.chass.utoronto.ca/epc.chwp/austin [accessed March 6, 2002].

Ang, Ien. 1998. "The Performance of the Sponge: Mass Communication Theory Enters the Postmodern World." In *The Media in Question: Popular Cultures and Public Interests,* edited by Kees Brants, Joke Hermes, and Liesbet van Zoonen. Thousand Oaks, Calif.: Sage.

Bakhtin, M. M. 1981. *The Dialogic Imagination.* Translated by Caryl Emerson and Michael Holmquist. Austin: University of Texas Press.

Barmossy, Gary, Soren Askegaard, and Michael Solomon. 2002. *Consumer Behaviour: A European Perspective.* Harrow, U.K.: Financial Times/Prentice Hall.

Barthes, Roland. 1977. "The Death of the Author." In *Image—Music—Text.* Translated by Stephen Heath. New York: Hill & Wang.

Baudrillard, Jean. 1983. *Simulations.* New York: Semiotext(e).

———. 1984. "On Nihilism." *On the Beach* 6 (spring): 38–39.

———. 1988. *America.* London: Verso.

———. 1993. "The Evil Demon of Images and the Precession of Simulacra." In *Postmodernism: A Reader,* edited by Thomas Docherty. New York: Columbia University Press.

Bauman, Zygmunt. 1992. *Intimations of Postmodernity.* New York: Routledge.

Berger, Arthur Asa. 1997. *Postmortem for a Postmodernist.* Walnut Creek, Calif.: AltaMira.

———. 1998. *The Postmodern Presence: Readings on Postmodernism in American Culture and Society.* Walnut Creek, Calif.: AltaMira.

———. 2002. *The Mass Comm Murders: Five Media Theorists Self-Destruct.* Lanham, Md.: Rowman & Littlefield.

Best, Steven, and Douglas Kellner. 1991. *Postmodern Theory: Critical Interrogations.* New York: Guilford.

Brants, Kees, Joke Hermes, and Liesbet van Zoonen, eds. 1998. *The Media in Question: Popular Cultures and Public Interests.* Thousand Oaks, Calif.: Sage.

Cashmore, Ellis, and Christ Rojek, eds. 1999. *Dictionary of Cultural Theorists.* London: Arnold.

Crook, Stephen, Jan Pakulski, and Malcolm Waters, eds. 1992. *Postmodernization: Change in Advanced Society.* London: Sage.

Denzin, Norman K. 1991. *Images of Postmodern Society: Social Theory and Contemporary Cinema.* London: Sage.

Derrida, Jacques. 1973. *Speech and Phenomena, and Other Essays on Husserl's Theory of Signs.* Evanston, Ill.: Northwestern University Press.

Featherstone, Mike. 1991. *Consumer Culture and Postmodernism.* London: Sage.

Foucault, Michel. 1973. *The Order of Things.* New York: Vintage.

Goffman, Erving. 1979. *Gender Advertisements.* New York: HarperCollins.

Gottdiener, Mark. 1995. *Postmodern Semiotics: Material Culture and the Forms of Postmodern Life.* Oxford, U.K.: Blackwell.

Handy, Bruce. 1989. "A *Spy* Guide to Post-modern Everything." *Utne Reader,* July–August, 1989, 61.

Harvey, David. 1989. *The Condition of Postmodernity.* Oxford, U.K.: Blackwell.

Hawthorn, Jeremy. 1998. *A Concise Glossary of Contemporary Literary Theory.* 3d ed. London: Arnold.

hooks, bell. "Postmodern Blackness." www.sas.upenn.edu/African_Studies/Articles_Gen/Postmodern_Blackness_18270.html.

Hudnut, J. 1985. *Architecture and the Spirit of Man.* Westport, Conn.: Greenwood.

Hutcheon, Linda. 1990. *A Poetics of Postmodernism: History, Theory, Fiction.* New York: Routledge.

———. 1997. "Theorizing Feminism and Postmodernity." www.english.ucsb.edu/faculty/ayliu/research/grandy-hutcheon [accessed March 15, 2002].

Huyssen, Andreas. 1986. *After the Great Divide: Modernism, Mass Culture, Postmodernism.* Bloomington: Indiana University Press.

Illouz, Eva. 1998. "The Lost Innocence of Love: Romance as a Postmodern Condition." *Theory, Culture, and Society* 15, nos. 3–4, 175–76.

Irvine, Martin. 1998. "The Postmodern, Postmodernism, Postmodernity: Approaches to Po-Mo." www.georgetown.edu/irvinem/technoculture/pomo.html [accessed December 28, 2001].

Jameson, Fredric. 1984. "Postmodernism, or The Cultural Logic of Late Capitalism." *New Left Review,* no. 146, July–August.

———. 1991. *Postmodernism, or The Cultural Logic of Late Capitalism.* Durham, N.C.: Duke University Press.

Jencks, Charles. 1977. *The Language of Post-Modern Architecture.* New York: Rizzoli.

———. 1991. "Postmodern vs. Late Modern." In *Zeitgeist in Babel: The Post-Modernist Controversy,* edited by Ingeborg Hoesterey. Bloomington: Indiana University Press.

Joseph, Sarah. 1998. *Interrogating Culture: Critical Perspectives on Contemporary Social Theory.* New Delhi: Sage.

Joyce, James. 1942. *Ulysses.* New York: Random House.

Keep, Christopher, Tim McLaughlin, and Robin Parmar. "Postmodernism and the Postmodern Novel." www.iath.virginia.edu/elab/hfl0256.html [accessed June 6, 2002].

Kristeva, Julia. 1986. "Stabat Mater." In *The Kristeva Reader,* edited by Julia Kristeva and Toril Moi. New York: Columbia University Press, 160–161.

Lehman, David. 2002. "The Questions of Postmodernism." www.zip.com.au/jtranter/jacket04/Lehman-postmod.html [accessed June 6, 2002].

Lodge, David. 1977. *The Modes of Modern Writing: Metaphor, Metonymy, and the Typology of Modern Literature.* London: Arnold.

Lyotard, Jean-François. 1984. *The Postmodern Condition: A Report on Knowledge.* Minneapolis: University of Minnesota Press.

McWilliams, Mark. 2002. "The Flavors of Postmodernity." www.people.virginia.edu/~mbm5w/papers/fusion.html [accessed March 18, 2002].

Musil, Robert. 1965. *The Man without Qualities.* vol. 1, *A Sort of Introduction The Like of It Now Happens (I).* New York: Capricorn.

Nehring, Neil. 1997. *Popular Music, Gender, and Postmodernism: Anger Is an Energy.* Thousand Oaks, Calif.: Sage.

Nietzsche, Friedrich. 1987. *The Will to Power.* Translated by R. Hollingdale and W. Kauffman. New York: Random House.

Perec, Georges. 1978. *Life: A User's Manual.* Translated by David Bellows. Boston: Godine.

Pynchon, Thomas. 1966. *The Crying of Lot 49.* New York: Bantam.

Rosenberg, Bernard, and David Manning White, eds. 1957. *Mass Culture.* Glencoe, Ill.: Free Press.

Safran, Marci. 1996. "Jameson, Jencks, and Juniors: Generation X as Critical Paradigm." *(Im)positions,* no. 1, December.

Salim, Majid. "A Study of Ridley Scott's *Blade Runner.*" www.majid-salim.co.uk/br/pa.html [accessed February 6, 2002].

Saussure, Ferdinand de. 1966. *Course in General Linguistics.* Translated by Wade Baskin. New York: McGraw-Hill.

Simons, Herbert W., and Michael Billig, eds. 1994. *After Postmodernism: Reconstructing Ideology Critique.* London: Sage.

Solomon, Jack. 1988. *The Signs of Our Time.* Los Angeles: Tarcher.

Solomon, Larry. "What Is Postmodernism?" www.azstarnet.com/~solo/postmod.htm [accessed November 18, 2001].

Sontag, Susan. 1969. *Against Interpretation.* New York: Laurel Books.

Tijssen, Lieteke van Vucht. 1990. "Women between Modernity and Postmodernity." In *Theories of Modernity and Postmodernity,* edited by Bryan S. Turner. London: Sage.

Toynbee, Arnold. 1947. *A Study of History* (abridgement of first seven vols.). New York: Oxford University Press.

Turner, Bryan S., ed. 1990. *Theories of Modernity and Postmodernity.* London: Sage.

Index

Cervantes, Miguel de, 86
Cézanne, Paul, 30
Cixous, Hélène, xvi, 54–55
Clinton, Hillary Rodham, 52
concepts: defined negatively, 32; oppositional aspects of American national identity, 33; purely differential, 32; role in feminist thought, 54–55; Saussure on, 12
Concise Glossary of Contemporary Literary Theory, 44
Condition of Postmodernity, 52
Consumer Culture and Postmodernism, 30
Continuous Life, 92
Coover, Robert, 36, 37
Crook, Stephen, 48
Crying of Lot 49, 37–39; postmodern aspects of, 39; and southern California culture, 39
Cummins, James, 92

DaVinci. *See* Leonardo da Vinci
Denzin, Norman K., xiii, 14–15
Derrida, Jacques, xiv, 34–35, 88
Descartes, René, 12
Dialogic Imagination, 47
dialogism: intertextuality and, 47; monologism and, 47
Dictionary of Cultural Theorists, viii
Disney, Walt: Disneyfication of world, 66–67; Disneyland and Disneyworld, 66; postmodernism and, 66–67; simulations and, 66–67
Docherty, Thomas, 56
Don Quixote, 86
Dornenburg, Andrew, 90
Durkheim, Émile, xi

Einstein, Albert, 98
Eliot, T. S., 30, 44, 86
Emerson, Ralph Waldo, 33

Faulkner, William, 30
Featherstone, Mike, 30–31
feminism: man/woman opposition and, 55; need for new representation of femininity, 20–21; postmodernism and, 18–19; relation to the maternal, 20–21
Finiger, Susan, 90
Finnegan's Wake, 42
Foucault, Michel, xiii, 12, 13, 46, 80–81
Freud, Sigmund, 20, 44
fusion food: inventor of term, 90; relation to postmodernism, 90–91; uniting traditions thought incompatible, 91
Fusion Food Cookbook, 90

Gender Advertisements, 76
Gide, André, 30
Godfather Part II, 92
Goffman, Erving, 76
Gottdiener, Mark, 73
gram: differance and meaning, 34–35; grammatology and, 34–35; new concept of writing, 34
Graves, Michael, 58, 98

Harvey, David, 44, 52
Hawthorn, Jeremy, 44
Hermes, Joke, 74
Herriman, George, 92
Hoesterey, Ingeborg, 58
Hollein, Hans, 58
hooks, bell, xiv, 51, 53
Hudnut, Joseph, 37
Hutcheon, Linda, xv, 18–19, 88
Huyssen, Andreas, xii
hyperdifferentiation: consumption and, 49; cultural fragmentation and, 48–49; postmodernism and, 48–49

tion, 3; role in culture studies, 80–81; role of images in, 24–25; romantic love and, 96–97; simulations and, 12–13, 56–57; social theorizing and, 14–15; therapy and, 94; ubiquitous aspects of, 14–15

Postmodernism, or The Cultural Logic of Late Capitalism, xv

Postmodernization: Change in Advanced Society, 48

Postmodern Theory: Critical Interrogations, 7

Potter, Dennis, 92

Pound, Ezra, 30, 90

Pride and Prejudice, 44

Pulp Fiction, 84

punk: lack of radicalizing power, 52–53; postmodernism and, 52–53; relation to authoritarianism, 52

Pynchon, Thomas, 37, 38–39, 86

Regulae, 12

Rilke, Rainer Maria, 30

Rocky, 84

Rojek, Chris, viii–ix

romantic love: affairs as postmodernist, 96–97; postmodernism and, 96–97; sex as consumption, 96–97

Rosenberg, Bernard, viii

Rothko, Mark, 98

Salim, Majid, 85

Sandison, Teri, 90

Saussure, Ferdinand de, ix, xiii, xiv, 32, 35, 55, 57, 73, 77, 101

Schoenberg, Arnold, 30, 98

Scitovsky, Tibor, 96

Seidelman, Susan, 36, 37

Shawver, Lois, 94–95

Shore, Lydia, 90

signs: meaning of signifieds can change, 72; relation between signfier and signified, 72–73; role of signifieds in consumer cultures, 72

Signs of Our Time, 8

Simons, Herbert W., 68

simulations: postmodernism and, 56–57; representations and, 56–57; stages in evolution of, 56

Singing Detective, 92

Solomon, Jack, xii, 8, 9

Solomon, Larry, 99, 101

Solomon, Michael, 79

Somervell, D. C., viii

Sontag, Susan, xiv, 60–61

Stern, Robert, 58

Stockhausen, Karlheinz, 98

Strand, Mark, 92

Stravinsky, Igor, 30, 98

Strinati, Dominic, 52

Survivor, 23

Suspects, 92

texts: importance of readers, 28–29; intertextuality and, 28–29

Theories of Modernity and Postmodernity, x

therapy: modernism and, 94–95; paralogy explained, 94–95; postmodernism and, 94–95

Thirty are better than one, 84

Thompson, David, 92

Toynbee, Arnold, viii

Turner, Bryan S., x, 77

Ulysses, 41, 42, 62–63

Valéry, Paul, 30

Venturi, Robert, 58

Void, 65

Vucht, Lieteke van, 77

About the Author

Arthur Asa Berger is professor emeritus of broadcast and electronic communication arts at San Francisco State University, where he has taught since 1965. He now defines himself as a postmodernist novelist, having written a number of comic academic mystery novels: *Postmortem for a Postmodernist, The Mass Comm Murders, Durkheim Is Dead*, and *The Hamlet Case*. (These books, in the best postmodern tradition, are also used as textbooks for their respective subjects—postmodernism, mass communication theory, sociological theory, and applied literary theory.) He has also written about forty nonfiction books on media, popular culture, and everyday life. (There are some who believe that everything he writes is fiction and that he just makes things up as he goes along, throwing in charts to fool social scientists.) Among his recent books are *Media Analysis Techniques* (2d ed.), *Bloom's Morning, Video Games: A Popular Culture Phenomenon,* and *The Agent in the Agency.* He has written a number of books on humor, including *An Anatomy of Humor, The Genius of the Jewish Joke,* and *Jewish Jesters.* His books have been translated into Italian, German, Swedish, Chinese, Korean, and, so it is rumored, Turkish, Indonesian, and Arabic. He is married, has two children, and lives in Mill Valley, California. His e-mail address is aberger@sfsu.edu.

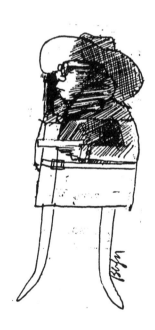

Exterior of Westin Bonaventure Hotel, Los Angeles. (Courtesy of Westin Bonaventure Hotel.)